The Mind of Economic Man

A

The Mind of Economic Man

An anthology compiled by
Denis Thomas

Quadrangle Books

Printed in England by Ditchling Press Ltd, Sussex, for the
publishers, Quadrangle Publications Ltd, Coach House,
Oakwood Close, Chislehurst, Kent

Contents

Publishers' Note
A line of text has inadvertently been repeated four lines from the foot of page 49 ('can throw . . . which'), and one line missed out in Item 408, the opening sentences of which should read: 'Capitalism has become so complicated that private initiative is insufficient to regulate it; the democratization of political power has made collective initiative imperative. There is, therefore, a new view of the state and of economic order.'

Foreword

The term Economic Man calls, perhaps, for brief explanation. It was first used, so far as I have been able to determine, at the end of the eighteenth century by Jeremy Bentham, whose writings helped to establish economics as philosophically—even culturally—respectable. The word 'economics' is not to be found in Johnson's Dictionary, and as a popular concept the notion that 'economy' could have anything to do with the human condition, much less with an academic discipline, is relatively modern. In looking for quotations from early commentators, philosophers and men of letters, I have had to suppose that many of them were in fact talking about economics, or Economic Man, long before those terms became attached to the causes and effects of social organization. Man's instincts for bettering himself, for getting ahead by working and scheming to improve his situation in life, is obviously older than the written word. There are glimmerings of a philosophical rationalization of this instinct in the earliest literature. So the term Economic Man is not altogether a misnomer when applied in retrospect over the three-hundred-year span of western civilization, even if its implications are becoming totally clear to us only in the mid-twentieth-century.

My selection of quotations does not presume either to be comprehensive or, in the political sense nowadays inseparable from economic opinion, to be balanced. The essence of an anthology is selectivity, and to make a choice is at the same time to make a judgement. The classical economists and their followers, who are conspicuous in these pages, established a canon which is antithetical to all 'reformist' economic opinion since Marx. This, however, does not invalidate what they said: on the contrary, given the subsequent experience of collectivist policies—in capitalist economies as well as in the socialist world—their principles seem to re-enter our lives with undiminished force. I have found no text which more sadly underlines the failure of Economic Man to live up to Utopian ideals than the two sentences in which Sir Thomas More urges that, since the rich are wicked and the poor are virtuous, laws ought to be passed forbidding anyone to own more than a certain amount of land, or to earn more than a certain amount of money.

Except where a chronological order has seemed appropriate, the arrangement of the extracts is designed to reinforce and complement neighbouring quotations. In addition to an occasional aphorism there are assorted examples of resounding nonsense by some of the best authorities. For the most part, however, the five hundred extracts have been chosen for the pertinence of what is said and for the quality of the author's mind.

This book owes its genesis to an idea originally discussed by a group of distinguished academics, none of whom was entirely clear how it could best be done. That it was done at all, and by a non-economist, is due to the thoughtful patronage of Shell.

DENIS THOMAS

I

Critique of Political Economy

[1] The city originates because we are not self-sufficient. . . . Or is there another origin of settlement in cities? Men gather into one settlement many helpers, since they need many things. . . . And when they share their goods with one another, the one giving, the other partaking, does not every one expect in this way to further his own interest? PLATO
The Republic, c. 460 B.C.

[2] The great art . . . of political oeconomy is first to adapt the different operations of it to the spirit, manners, habits and customs of the people, and afterwards to model these circumstances so as to be able to introduce a set of new and more useful institutions.

The principal object of this science is to secure a certain fund of subsistance for all the inhabitants, to obviate every circumstance which may render it precarious; to provide everything necessary for supplying the wants of the society and to employ the inhabitants (supposing them to be freemen) in such a manner as naturally to create reciprocal relations and dependencies between them so as to make their several interests lead them to supply one another with their reciprocal wants. SIR JAMES STEUART
Inquiry into the Principles of Political Oeconomy, 1767

[3] Does Political Economy condemn those efforts of men to make their industry more productive and profitable? Does she affirm anywhere that human nature has reached perfection? Quite the contrary. I believe that there is no science which demonstrates more clearly that society is still in its infancy. FREDERIC BASTIAT
Harmonies of Political Economy, 1860

[4] Political Economy or Economics is a study of mankind in the ordinary business of life; it examines that part of

individual and social action which is most closely connected with the attainment and with the use of the material requisites of well-being. ALFRED MARSHALL

Opening words of *Principles of Economics*, 1890

[5] The economist, when he does use a word out of its ordinary meaning, is usually doing one of two things. He is either narrowing it to something less than it means to ordinary people, or broadening it to something more. In either case the results are apt to be unfortunate for Economic Theory, as well as misleading to the public.

G. D. H. COLE

Economic Tracts for the Times, 1932

[6] The enlightened student of political economy and of society will take care to assume nothing as to the economic forces except the constant pressure which they bring to bear upon men's action and their absolute moral and social indifference. PHILIP H. WICKSTEED

The Common Sense of Political Economy, 1910

[7] Wonder, Carlyle declared, is the beginning of philosophy. It is not wonder, but rather the social enthusiasm which revolts from the sordidness of mean streets and the joylessness of withered lives, that is the beginning of economic science. ARTHUR CECIL PIGOU

The Economics of Welfare (3rd edn.), 1929

[8] It is now sixteen or seventeen years since I saw the Queen of France, then the Dauphiness, at Versailles; and surely never lighted on this orb a more delightful vision. . . . Little did I dream that I should live to see disasters fallen upon her in a nation of gallant men, in a nation of men of honour, and of cavaliers. I thought ten thousand swords must have leapt

from their scabbards to avenge even a look that threatened her with insult. But the age of chivalry is gone. That of sophisters, economists and calculators has succeeded; and the glory of Europe is extinguished for ever.

EDMUND BURKE
Reflections on the Revolution in France, 1790

[9] I do not see that there can exist a code of laws concerning political economy distinct and separate from all other codes. The collection of laws upon this subject would only be a mass of imperfect shreds, drawn without distinction from the whole body of laws. JEREMY BENTHAM
'View of a Code of Laws', *Works*, 1843

[10] Not that Political Economy is without its poetry. There is poetry wherever order and harmony exist. But it is in the results, not in the demonstrations. It is brought out, not created. FREDERIC BASTIAT
Harmonies of Political Economy, 1860

[11] Man cannot live without some economic theology—without some rationalisation of the abstract and seemingly inchoate arrangements which provide him with his livelihood. JOHN KENNETH GALBRAITH
American Capitalism, 1952

[12] If economists could get themselves thought of as humble, competent people, on a level with dentists, that would be splendid. JOHN MAYNARD KEYNES
Essays in Persuasion, 1931

[13] It will be remembered that the seventy translators of the Septuagint were shut up in seventy separate rooms with the Hebrew text and brought out with them, when they

emerged, seventy identical translations. Would the same miracle be vouchsafed if seventy multiple correlators were shut up with the same statistical material? And anyhow, I suppose, if each had a different economist perched on his *a priori*, that would make a difference to the outcome.

JOHN MAYNARD KEYNES
'Professor Tinbergen's Method', *The Economic Journal*, 1939–40

[14] For many years I have been employed as a teacher of theoretical economics; I would like to believe that I earn my living honestly, but I often have doubts.

JOAN ROBINSON
'Teaching Economics', *Collected Economic Papers*, 1965

[15] I don't regret my education. I don't regret it in my present position as a business man. My old teacher Cannan used to say that no pupil of the London School of Economics ever died in the workhouse; and I believe that, historically speaking, that is true.

LORD ROBBINS
At an I.E.A. dinner, January 1966

[16] Political economy is at once a science and an art. The value of the science has for its efficient cause and measure its subserviency to the art.

According to the principle of utility, in every branch of the art of legislation, the object or end in view is the production of the maximum of happiness in a given time in the community in question.

In the instance of this branch of the art, the object or end in view is the producing that maximum of happiness in so far as the other more general end is promoted by the production of the maximum of wealth and the maximum of population.

JEREMY BENTHAM
An Institute of Political Economy, 1801–04

[17] It appears to me impossible but that the increase of intelligence of education, and of love of independence among the working classes must be attended with the corresponding growth of the good sense which manifests itself in provident habits of conduct, and that population, therefore, will bear gradually diminishing ratio to capital and employment. JOHN STUART MILL
Principles of Political Economy, 1848

[18] John Stuart Mill
By a mighty effort of will
Overcame his natural bonhomie
And wrote 'Principles of Political Economy'.
EDMUND CLERIHEW BENTLEY
Biography for Beginners, 1905

[19] Economists have a singular method of procedure. There are only two kinds of institutions for them, artificial and natural. . . . In this they resemble the theologians, who likewise establish two kinds of religion. Every religion which is not theirs is an invention of men, while their own is an emanation from God. KARL MARX
The Poverty of Philosophy, 1846

[20] The economist is treated by the public rather like a quack doctor, or like a priest of an ancient religion surviving into an age of scepticism. Generally he can be treated with amused contempt, as an unscientific person who talks in mysteries or who (if he ventures to make a clear, definite statement) will at once be contradicted by a fellow-economist. But when people can find no relief from the pains of economic life, and the fears of the unknown gather round, they return to the economist as Expert, invest him

with authority in a Council or a Committee or a government office, and wait for a report which will ease the pains and remove the fears.

This is a misuse of experts. . . . The little orphan Neddy and the infant Nick can both, over the years, achieve a modest usefulness, but they represent no addition to the intellectual resources of the country, and offer no assurance that unpleasant decisions will be easier to take. The wise will keep their hopes small.

C. F. CARTER
District Bank Review, September 1962

[21] I think I may fairly make two postulata. First, that food is necessary to the existence of man. Secondly, that the passion between the sexes is necessary and will remain nearly in its present state. . . . Assuming, then, my postulata as granted, I say that the power of population is indefinitely greater than the power of the earth to produce subsistence for man. Population, when unchecked, increases in a geometrical ratio. Subsistence only increases in an arithmetical ratio. A slight acquaintance with numbers will show the immensity of the first power in comparison with the second.

THOMAS ROBERT MALTHUS
An Essay in the Principle of the Population, 1798

[22] He gave it for his opinion, that whoever could make two ears of corn or two blades of grass grow upon a spot of ground where only one grew before, would deserve better of mankind, and do more essential service to his country, than the whole race of politicians put together.

JONATHAN SWIFT
Gulliver's Travels, 1726

[23] Turgot and Adam Smith were beyond all comparison more sincere guides to earthly prosperity than St. Paul. If

they could have foreseen the history of the practical application of their principles in the nineteenth century in England they would have recoiled in horror, just as Karl Marx would have recoiled if he had been foreshown what happened in Russia from 1917 to 1921 through the action of able and devoted men who made his writings their Bible. Good people are the very devil sometimes....

BERNARD SHAW
The Intelligent Woman's Guide to Socialism and Capitalism, 1928

[24] O let us love our occupations,
Bless the squire and his relations,
Live upon our daily rations,
And always know our proper stations.

CHARLES DICKENS
The Chimes, 1845

[25] Three great primary inventions have given stability to society beside the large number of others which have enriched and adorned it. These three are: (1) the invention of writing, which alone gives a man the power of handing down without alteration his laws, his contracts, his annals and his discoveries. (2) That of money, which binds together all relations in civilized societies. The third and last, which brings to our age and of which our descendants will enjoy the fruit, is derived from the other two and completes each of them equally by perfecting their object: it is the discovery of the Economic Table which, becoming henceforth the universal interpreter, embraces and harmonises all the correlative fractions or proportions which should enter into every general calculation of the economic order.

HONORE GABRIEL MIRABEAU
Philosophie Rurale, 1766

[26] Economics is not a subject that can be learned, like mathematics, as a series of propositions that follow from one another with the neatness of a Chinese box. It is much more like medicine, compounded of imperfect knowledge, worldly wisdom, obscure jargon and scientific analysis. The student of medicine learns many things about the human body that are meant to improve his powers of diagnosis; but he can make mistakes, and his patients can disagree with him, sometimes quite violently. The student of economics is in much the same position. He learns a great deal about the economy of his country and of other countries. But since he is studying things with which everybody is familiar, such as production, trade, and income, and his conclusions about these things do not usually rest on an infallible logic beyond the comprehension of the ordinary man, he is wise to get used to the idea, right at the beginning, but there is room for disagreement in economic diagnosis, and that people will disagree with him. ALEC CAIRNCROSS

Introduction to Economics, 1960

[27] I believe myself to be writing a book on economic theory which will largely revolutionize—not, I suppose, at once but in the course of the next ten years—the way the world thinks about economic problems.

JOHN MAYNARD KEYNES

Letter to Bernard Shaw, 1935

[28] The ideas of economists and political philosophers, both when they are right and when they are wrong, are more powerful than is commonly understood, indeed the world is ruled by little else. Practical men, who believe themselves to be quite exempt from any intellectual influences, are usually the slaves of some defunct economist.

Madmen in authority, who hear voices in the air, are distilling their frenzy from some academic scribbler of a few years back. I am sure that the power of vested interests is vastly exaggerated compared with the gradual encroachment of ideas. Not, indeed, immediately, but after a certain interval; for in the field of economic and political philosophy there are not many who are influenced by new theories after they are twenty-five or thirty years of age, so that the ideas which civil servants and politicians and even agitators apply to current events are not likely to be the newest. But, soon or late, it is ideas, not vested interests, which are dangerous for good or evil. JOHN MAYNARD KEYNES
The General Theory of Employment, Interest, and Money, 1936

[29] *Laissez-faire:* in classical economic theory a doctrine based on the proposition that the economic affairs of society will in the main take care of themselves if neither the state nor any other body armed with authority attempts to interfere with their working as determined by the individual actions of men.
Everyman's Dictionary of Economics, 1965

[30] In recent years *laissez-faire* has come to be used as a term of abuse, and totalitarian writers have not been slow to take advantage of this to stigmatize any policy whatever which in any way smacks of freedom. I await with virtual certainty the emergence of the term '*laissez-faire* collectivism' to smear those socialist plans that would at least allow some freedom in the sphere of consumption. LORD ROBBINS
Politics and Economics, 1963

[31] The study which lately in England has been called Political Economy is in reality nothing more than the

investigation of some accidental phenomena of modern commercial operations, nor has it been true in its investigation even of these. It has no connection whatever with political economy, as understood and treated of by the great thinkers of past ages; and as long as its unscholarly and undefined statements are allowed to pass under the same name—and chiefly the words of Plato, Xenophon, Cicero and Bacon—must be nearly useless to mankind.

JOHN RUSKIN
Munera Pulveris, 1880

[32] The real science of political economy, which has yet to be distinguished from the bastard science, as medicine from witchcraft and astronomy from astrology, is that which teaches nations to desire and labour for the things that lead to life; and which teaches them to scorn and destroy the things that lead to destruction.

JOHN RUSKIN
'Ad Valorem', *Unto This Last*, 1862

[33] The subject treated by the Political Economist, using that term in the limited sense in which we apply it, is not Happiness, but Wealth; his premises consist of a very few general propositions, the result of observation, or consciousness, and scarcely requiring proof, or even formal statement, which almost every man, as soon as he hears them, admits as familiar to his thoughts, or at least as included in his previous knowledge; and his inferences are nearly as general, and, if he has reasoned correctly, as certain, as his premises....

But his conclusions, whatever be their generality and their truth, do not authorize him in adding a single syllable of advice. That privilege belongs to the writer or the statesman who considered all the causes which may promote or impede the general welfare of those whom he addresses, not to the theorist who has considered only one, though among the most important, of those causes. The business of a Political Economist is neither to recommend nor to dissuade, but to state general principles, which it is fatal to neglect, but neither advisable, nor perhaps practicable, to use as the sole, or even the principal, guides in the actual conduct of affairs.

NASSAU WILLIAM SENIOR
An Outline of the Science of Political Economy, 1836

[34] Confounding the Science of Political Economy with the Sciences and Arts to which it is subservient, has seduced Economists sometimes to undertake inquiries too vague to lead to any pratical results, and sometimes to pursue the legitimate objects of the Science by means unfit for their attainment. To their extended view of the objects of Political Economy is to be attributed the undue importance which many Economists have ascribed to the collection of facts, and their neglect of the far more important process of reasoning accurately from the facts before them.

NASSAU WILLIAM SENIOR
An Outline of the Science of Political Economy, 1836

[35] Among the delusions which at different periods have possessed themselves of the minds of large masses of the human race, perhaps the most curious—certainly the least creditable—is the modern soi-distant science of political economy, based on the idea that an advantageous code of social action may be determined irrespectively of the influence of social affection.

JOHN RUSKIN
'The Roots of Honour', *Unto This Last*, 1862

[36] Political Economy . . . is a very difficult thing; something

altogether more abstruse and difficult, as well as more conclusive, than that which many of those who rush in upon it have a notion of. It is an abstract science which labours under a special hardship. Those who are conversant with its abstractions are usually without a true contact with its facts; those who are in contact with its facts have usually little sympathy with and little cognizance of its abstractions. Literary men who write about it are constantly using what a great teacher calls 'unreal words'—that is, they are using expressions with which they have no complete vivid picture to correspond. They are like physiologists who have never dissected; like astronomers who have never seen the stars; and, in consequence, just when they seem to be reasoning at their best, their knowledge of the facts falls short.

WALTER BAGEHOT
Economic Studies, 1888

[37] Economics relates in the main to man's attitude to the purchasable goods of the world, and therefore it is imperative to remind ourselves from time to time that all the goods of this world are not of such a kind. Indeed, it is the impalpable subjective things in life, without a price, which give to exchangeable goods their value. We cannot value books without culture, nor pictures without taste.

SIR SYDNEY CHAPMAN
Political Economy (11th imp.), 1945

[38] An economist whose work lies in a region apparently remote, so long as it is real and serious and not a mere building of cheap toys, is no less entitled than one who stands closer to the detail of actual life, to regard himself as a potential gardener of fruit.

ARTHUR CECIL PIGOU
Economics in Practice, 1936

[39] The bitter argument between economists and human beings has ended in the conversion of the economists.

ARNOLD TOYNBEE
Lectures on the Industrial Revolution, 1884

[40] A science of economics must be developed before a science of politics can be logically formulated. Essentially, economics is the science of determining whether the interests of human beings are harmonious or antagonistic. This must be known before a science of politics can be formulated to determine the proper functions of government.

FREDERIC BASTIAT
The Law, 1850

[41] The best and safest method of philosophizing seems to be, first to enquire diligently into the properties of things, and of establishing those properties by experiments, and then to proceed slowly to hypotheses for the explanation of them. For hypotheses should be subservient only in explaining them; unless so far as they may furnish experiments. For if the possibility of hypotheses is to be the test of truth and reality of things, I see not how certainty can be obtained in any science. . . .

SIR ISAAC NEWTON
Philosophical Transactions, c. 1687

[42] The economic structure of society always forms the real basis from which, in the last analysis, is to be explained the whole superstructure of legal and political institutions as well as the religious and other conceptions.

FREDERICK ENGELS
Anti-Dühring, 1845

[43] Political Economy . . . assumes a sort of human nature

such as we see everywhere around us, and again it simplifies that nature; it looks at one part of it only. Dealing with matters of 'business', it assumes that man is actuated only by motives of business. It assumes that every man who makes anything, makes it for money, that he always makes that which brings him in most at least cost, and that he will make it in the way that will produce most and spend least; it assumes that every man who buys, buys with his whole heart, and that he who sells, sells with his whole heart, each wanting to gain all possible advantage. Of course we know that this is not so, that men are not like this; but we assume it for simplicity's sake, as an hypothesis. And this deceives many excellent people, for from deficient education they have very indirect ideas what an abstract science is.

WALTER BAGEHOT
Economic Studies, 1879

[44] Economic theory is the theory of an orderly and reasonable world, a world with a concerted interchange of knowledge, a world where actions are pre-reconciled by the great market computer, and a world where what we intend is what will happen. . . . Economics is about order.

G. L. S. SHACKLE
The Years of High Theory, 1967

[45] 'Annual income twenty pounds, annual expenditure nineteen nineteen six, result happiness. Annual income twenty pounds, annual expenditure twenty pounds ought and six, result misery.'

CHARLES DICKENS
Mr Micawber in *David Copperfield*, 1849–50

[46] As Einstein stated, one single new fact could suffice to invalidate the whole theory of relativity. Thus, relativity

is in this sense shown to be of exceptionally fine structure. . . . What economic theory or 'law' would now be, or has ever been, overthrown by one single new fact?

OSKAR MORGENSTERN
On the Accuracy of Economic Observations (2nd edn.), 1963

[47] Man's brain has got no bigger but it buzzes more.

WINSTON CHURCHILL
1874–1965

[48] If the economists are correct, as they may be, in warning us that the amazing outburst of riches which took place in the nineteenth century is an episode which is over; if the period of increasing returns is ended and the period of diminishing returns has begun . . . then it is all the more necessary that the principles on which the economic order is founded should justify themselves to the consciences of decent men.

R. H. TAWNEY
The Acquisitive Society, 1921

[49] Economists may have come to realize—very rightly, in my judgment—that *as economists* they have nothing to say on the true ends of life; and that their propositions concerning what *is* or what *can be* involve in themselves no propositions concerning what *ought to be*.

LORD ROBBINS
Politics and Economics, 1963

[50] It is not that the quality of British economics, or economists, has sunk and now stands lower than in the past or than in other, less afflicted, countries. On the contrary, judged by the numbers of its professional practitioners and its lay addicts, economics was never more flourishing. The voice of academic economists was never louder and was

never heard with greater awe. Nor is there much wrong about the quality of the economists themselves. . . .

What is more questionable are the standards themselves, or to be more exact, the professional qualifications and attitudes which the economists bring, and are expected to bring, to their governmental and journalistic jobs. Are the contents of modern economics, the ideas with which the economists operate as relevant to the economic problems of our age as they and their public believe? Have they with their models, measurements and forecasts, helped the economic recovery, or have they, on the contrary, aggravated Britain's predicament by misdirecting the attention of the government and the public?

I am afraid my answer to these questions must go against the economists. MICHAEL M. POSTAN

'A Plague of Economists', *Encounter*, January 1968

[51] Economics is concerned with the *means* to secure *ends* which are set by men and women. Men and women allow politicians their power; and those politicians decide the *ends* for the people who give them their power. Men and women decide, acquiesce in, or tolerate political decisions, laws and rules. No economist, no businessman, decides and sets those rules. Yet no politician can make prosperity arrive if his nation's—or the world's—legal and political framework is not favourable to savings, to investment, to co-operation, competition and trade, to good management, and good industrial relations, and thus to the lowering of costs.

Nations, like individuals, get the kind of life they are prepared to organize and work for. Prosperity comes quickest by freely pulling together. That remains as true for a family as it does for a nation, and for the whole family of nations in the world. GRAHAM HUTTON

All Capitalists Now, 1960

[52] It may sound noble to say: damn economics, let us build up a decent world—but it is, in fact, merely irresponsible. With our world as it is, with everyone convinced that the material conditions here or there must be improved, our only chance of building a decent world is that we can continue to improve the general level of wealth. The one thing modern democracy will not bear without cracking is the necessity of a substantial lowering of the standards of living in peace time or even prolonged stationariness of its economic conditions. F. A. HAYEK

The Road to Serfdom, 1944

[53] Boswell: 'So, Sir, you laugh at schemes of political improvement.' Johnson: 'Why, Sir, most schemes of political improvement are very laughable things.'

JAMES BOSWELL

Life of Johnson, 1793

[54] We have hitherto lived upon Expedients, which in time will certainly destroy any Constitution, whether Civil or Natural; and there was no Country in Christendom had less Occasion for them, than ours. We have dieted a Healthy Body into a Consumption, by plying it with Physick, instead of Food.... JONATHAN SWIFT

The Conduct of the Allies, 1711

[55] The economist needs the three great intellectual faculties, perception, imagination, and reason: and most of all he needs imagination, to put him on the track of those

visible events which are remote or lie below the surface, and of those effects of visible causes which are remote or lie below the surface....

Economic studies call for and develop the faculty of sympathy, and especially that rare sympathy which enables people to put themselves in the place, not only of their comrades but also of other classes. ALFRED MARSHALL
Principles of Economics, 1890

[56] Certain modern theoretical economists have gone so far as to say that it is impossible to compare the level of income between two communities or between two individuals, or even between the same individual at different times; in other words, they deny the existence of any objectively measurable economic welfare (and incidentally provide themselves with a magnificent excuse for avoiding any study whatever of realistic and quantitative economics). I do not think that exponents of this view realize quite what an intellectual anarchy they will let loose if their theories are adopted. Deprive economics of the concept of welfare and what have you left? Nothing: except possibly the theory of the trade cycle, where all values may be capable of expression in money terms without the introduction of the concept of welfare. Even in this case you might be left in great doubts as to whether even the trade-cycle problem is worth solving. COLIN CLARK
The Conditions of Economic Progress, 1940

[57] The economist, if he has wide enough knowledge and is a shrewd judge of human nature and social institutions may venture tentative forecasts. But he is asking for trouble if he is too dogmatic about the accuracy of his predictions. Significantly enough, the foremost economic and financial

expert in post-war Thailand rejoiced in the appropriate name of Prince Dam Rong. J. W. NISBET
'A Political Economist's Apologia', *Economic Age*, November 1968

[58] As every individual . . . endeavours as much as he can both to employ his capital in the support of domestic industry, and so to direct that industry that its produce may be of the greatest value; every individual necessarily labours to render the annual revenue of the society as great as he can. He generally, indeed, neither intends to promote the public interest, nor knows how much he is promoting it. By preferring the support of domestic to that of foreign industry, he intends only his own security; and by directing that industry in such a manner as its produce may be of the greatest value, he intends only his own gain, and he is in this, as in many other cases, led by an invisible hand to promote an end which was no part of his intention. Nor is it always the worse for the society that it was no part of it. By pursuing his own interest he frequently promotes that of the society more effectually than when he really intends to promote it. I have never known much good done by those who affected to trade for the public good. It is an affectation, indeed, not very common among merchants, and very few words need be employed in dissuading them from it.

ADAM SMITH
The Wealth of Nations, 1776

[59] Under a system of perfectly free commerce, each country naturally devotes its capital and labour to such employments as are most beneficial to each. This pursuit of individual advantage is admirably connected with the universal good of the whole. By stimulating industry, by rewarding

ingenuity, and by using most efficaciously the peculiar powers bestowed by nature, it distributes labour most effectively and most economically: while, by increasing the general mass of productions, it diffuses general benefit and binds together by one common tie of interest and intercourse, the universal society of nations throughout the civilized world. DAVID RICARDO

The Principles of Political Economy and Taxation (3rd edn.), 1821

[60] Adam Smith completed the *Wealth of Nations* in 1776, and our English Political Economy is therefore just a hundred years old. In that time it has had a wonderful effect. The life of almost everyone in England—perhaps of everyone—is different and better in consequence of it. The whole commercial policy of the country is not so much founded on it as instinct with it. Ideas which are paradoxes everywhere else in the world are accepted axioms here as results of it. No other form of political philosophy has ever had one thousandth part of the influence on us; its teachings have settled down into the common sense of the nation, and have become irreversible. WALTER BAGEHOT

Economic Studies, 1888

[61] There can be no doubt that, in the broad sweep of history, the English Classical School from its beginnings in the philosophic speculations of Hume and Smith down to the very practical preoccupations of Senior and the Benthamites, must be regarded in its attitude to policy as a school of economic and social reform. . . . I do not believe that an unprejudiced reading of any of the works of the Classical authors can lead to any conclusion but that the scientific part of these works . . . was something which had a

status and a momentum of its own, subject to the general tests of scientific inquiry and acquiring as time went on a coherence and force which gave it, as it were, independent authority when they turned to considerations of policy.

LIONEL ROBBINS
The Theory of Economic Policy in English Classical Political Economy, 1952

[62] I find myself moved, not for the first time, to remind contemporary economists that the classical teaching embodied some permanent truths of great significance, which we are liable today to overlook because we associate them with other doctrines which we cannot now accept without much qualification. There are in these matters deep undercurrents at work, natural forces, one can call them, or even the invisible hand, which are operating towards equilibrium. If it were not so, we could not have got on even so well as we have for many decades past. The United States is becoming a high-living, high-cost country beyond any previous experience. Unless their internal, as well as their external, economic life is to become paralysed by the Midas touch, they will discover ways of life which, compared with the ways of the less fortunate regions of the world, must tend towards, and not away from, external equilibrium.

Admittedly, if the classical medicine is to work, it is essential that import tariffs and export subsidies should not progressively offset its influence. It is for this reason that one is entitled to draw some provisional comfort from the present mood of the American Administration and, as I judge it, of the American people also, as embodied in the *Proposals for Consideration by an International Conference on Trade and Employment*. We have here sincere and thoroughgoing proposals, advanced on behalf of the United States, expressly directed towards creating a system which allows the classical medicine to do its work. It shows how much modernist stuff, gone wrong and turned sour and silly, is circulating in our system, also incongruously mixed, it seems, with age-old poisons, that we should have given so doubtful a welcome to this magnificent, objective approach which a few years ago we should have regarded as offering incredible promise of a better scheme of things.

JOHN MAYNARD KEYNES
'The Balance of Payments in the United States', *Economic Journal*, June 1946. (The last article Keynes wrote.)

II

The Profit Motive

[63] It is an undeniable maxim that every one by the light of nature and reason will do that which makes for his greatest advantage. . . . The advancement of private persons will be the advantage of the public. JOSEPH LEE, 1656

Quoted in Tawney, *Religion and the Rise of Capitalism*

[64] The love of lucre, though sometimes carried to a ridiculous, sometimes to a vicious excess, is the grand cause of prosperity to all states. EDMUND BURKE

1729–1797

[65] [The landlords] grow richer, as it were, in their sleep, without working, risking, or economizing.

JOHN STUART MILL

Principles of Political Economy, 1848

[66] When every man aims at absolute ownership of all the property he can get, be there never so great an abundance of goods, it is all shared by a handful who leave the rest in poverty. It generally happens that the one class pre-eminently deserves the lot of the other, for the rich are greedy, unscrupulous, and useless, while the poor are well-behaved, simple, and by their daily industry more beneficial to the commonwealth than to themselves. . . . A statute might be made that no person should hold more than a certain amount of land and that no person should have a monetary income beyond that permitted by law.

SIR THOMAS MORE

Utopia, 1516

[67] He said, 'A man of noble birth went on a long journey abroad, to be appointed king and then return. But first he called ten of his servants and gave them a pound each,

saying, "Trade with this while I am away". His fellow-citizens hated him, and they sent a delegation on his heels to say, "We do not want this man as our king". However, back he came as king, and sent for the servants to whom he had given the money, to see what profit each had made. The first came and said, "Your pound, sir, has made ten more". "Well done," he replied; "you are a good servant. You have shown yourself trustworthy in a very small matter, and you shall have charge of ten cities." The second came and said, "Your pound, sir, has made five more"; and he was told, "You, too, take charge of five cities". The third came and said, "Here is your pound, sir; I kept it put away in a handkerchief. I was afraid of you, because you are a hard man: you draw out what you never put in and reap what you did not sow." "You rascal!" he replied: 'I will judge you by your own words. You knew, did you, that I am a hard man, that I draw out what I never put in, and reap what I did not sow? They why did you not put my money on deposit, and I could have claimed it with interest when I came back?" Turning to his attendants he said, "Take the pound from him and give it to the man with ten". "But sir", they replied, "he has ten already." "I tell you", he went on, "the man who has will always be given more; but the man who has not will forfeit even what he has. But as for those enemies of mine who did not want me for their king, bring them here and slaughter them in my presence."

Luke 19, i–xxvii. *New English Bible*

[68] The uniform, constant, and uninterrupted effort of every man to better his condition, the principle from which public and national, as well as private opulence is originally derived, is frequently powerful enough to maintain the

natural progress of things toward improvement, in spite of both the extravagance of government and of the greatest errors of administration.

. . . It is the highest impertinence and presumption, therefore, in kings and ministers, to pretend to watch over the economy of private people, and to restrain their expense, either by sumptuary laws, or by prohibiting the importation of foreign luxuries. They are themselves, always and without any exception, the greatest spendthrifts in the society. Let them look well after their own expense and they may safely trust private people with theirs. If their own extravagance does not ruin the state, that of their subjects never will.

ADAM SMITH
The Wealth of Nations, 1776

[69] Suppose the butchers are on one side and the buyers on the other. The price of meat will be settled after some higgling; and one pound of beef will be nearly in value to one piece of money as all the beef exposed for sale in the market is to all the money which has been brought there to buy beef.

This proportion is regulated by higgling. The butcher holds up his price on the strength of the number of buyers whom he sees; the buyers on their side offer less according as they think the butcher will have less sale: the price set by some is commonly followed by others. Some bargainers are cleverer at making their merchandise go off well, others more expert at crying it down. Although this method of fixing prices on the market has no exact or geometrical foundation, since it often depends on the eagerness or on the slackness of a small number of buyers or of sellers, yet it seems unlikely that the end could be arrived at by any more convenient way. It is always the case that the quantity of buyers is the basis on which the actual market prices are fixed, or believed to be fixed, and that in general these prices do not differ much from the intrinsic value.

RICHARD CANTILLON
Essai sur la Nature du Commerce en Général, 1755

[70] The value of all wares arises from their use; things of no use have no value; as the English phrase is, They are good for nothing.

The use of things are to supply the wants and necessities of man. There are two general wants that mankind is born with; the wants of the body and the wants of the mind; to supply these two necessities all things under the sun become useful and therefore have a value. . . .

The price of wares is the present value; and ariseth by computing the occasions or use for them with the quantity to serve that occasion; for the value of things depending on the use of them, the overplus of those wares which are more than can be used, become worth nothing; so that plenty in respect of the occasion, makes things cheap; and scarcity, dear.

There is no fixed price or value of anything for the wares of trades; the animals and vegetables of the earth depend on the influence of heaven, which sometimes causes murrains, dearth, famine, and sometimes years of great plenty; therefore the value of things must accordingly alter. Besides, the use of most things being to supply the wants of the mind and not the necessities of the body, and those wants most of them proceeding from imagination, the mind changeth; the things grow out of use, and so lose their value. . . .

But the market is the best judge of value; for by the concourse of buyers and sellers the quantity of wares and the occasion for them are best known; things are just worth so much as they can be sold for, according to the old rule, *valet quantum potest.* NICHOLAS BARBON

Discourse of Trade, 1690

[71] The ground of all price must be some *fitness* in the things to yield some use or pleasure in life; without this they can be of no value. But this being presupposed, the prices of things will be in a compound proportion of the *demand* for them and the *difficulty* in acquiring them. The *demand* will be in proportion to the numbers who are wanting them, or their necessity to life. The difficulty may be occasioned many ways: if the quantities of them in the world be small; if any accidents make the quantity less than ordinary; if much toil is required in producing them, or much ingenuity or a more elegant genius in the artists; if the persons employed about them according to the custom of the country are men in high account, and live in a more splendid manner; for the expense of this must be defrayed by the higher profits of their labours, and few can be thus maintained.

Some goods of the highest use yet have either no price or but a small one. If there is such plenty in nature that they are acquired almost without any labour, they have no price: if they may be acquired by easy common labour they are of small price. Such is the goodness of God to us that the most useful and necessary things are generally very plentiful and easily acquired.

Other things of great use have no price, either because they are naturally destined for community, or cannot come

into commerce but as appendages of something else, the price of which may be increased by them through they cannot be separately estimated. FRANCIS HUTCHESON
Introduction to Moral Philosophy, 1747

[72] Stockjobber: a low wretch who gets money by buying and selling shares in the funds. SAMUEL JOHNSON
The *Dictionary*, 1755

[73] Generally speaking, there is no one who knows what is for your interest so well as yourself—no one who is disposed with so much ardour and constancy to pursue it.
JEREMY BENTHAM
Manual of Political Economy, 1825

[74] All progress is based upon a universal innate desire on the part of every organism to live beyond its income.
SAMUEL BUTLER
Notebooks, 1912 (posthumous)

[75] The desire of self-preservation is called a natural propensity, that is to say is regarded with approbation. The desire of gain is a propensity not less natural, but in this case, although more useful, it is not regarded with the same approbation. This is a mischievous prejudice, but it exists and it is therefore necessary to combat its influence. We must treat opinions as we find them, and not act as though they were what they ought to be. This is not the only instance in which it is necessary to put a constraint upon men's inclinations, that they may be at liberty to follow them. JEREMY BENTHAM
The Psychology of Economic Man, c. 1799

[76] The commodity is . . . sold precisely for what it is worth,

or for what it really costs the person who brings it to market; for though in common language what is called the prime cost of any commodity does not comprehend the profit of the person who is to sell it again, yet if he sells it at a price which does not allow him the ordinary rate of profit in his neighbourhood, he is evidently the loser by the trade; since by employing his stock in some other way he might have made that profit. His profit, besides, is his revenue, the proper fund of his subsistence. As, while he is preparing and bringing the goods to market, he advances to his workmen their wages, or their subsistence, so he advances to himself, in the same manner, his own subsistence, which is generally suitable to the profit which he may reasonably expect from the sale of his goods. Unless they yield him this profit, therefore, they do not repay him what they may very properly be said to have really cost him.

ADAM SMITH
The Wealth of Nations, 1776

[77] When in doubt, expand.

A. C. PIGOU
The Times, 21 February, 1933

[78] Opulence, though so nearly of kin to wealth, or rather for that very reason, requires to be distinguished from it: opulence is relative wealth, relation being had to population: it is the ratio of wealth to population. Quantity of wealth being given, the degree of opulence is therefore not directly, but inversely, as the population, i.e. as the degree of populousness—as the number of those who are to share in it: the fewer the sharers, the larger is each one's share.

JEREMY BENTHAM
An Institute of Political Economy, 1801–04

[79] The more equalitarian the general living conditions of the society are, the smaller will be the incentives that will be needed. This follows from the fact that a small addition to a relatively small income is worth more in terms of human satisfaction than a larger addition to a larger income, as well as from the fact that, when no one is rich, there is much less inducement to seek to become rich than when society is divided into widely separated income classes enjoying very different degrees of power and prestige. To discover how much is necessary, under any particular set of conditions, is a matter of trial and adjustment in the light of experience, not for abstract theorising. All that can be said with confidence is that the magnitude of the incentives offered at the top end of the scale in capitalist societies is a by-product of the class system and is not the response to any fundamental law of economics or of human nature. G. D. H. COLE
The Intelligent Man's Guide to the Post-War World, 1947

[80] In political economy, one of the most copious sources of error is a blind and sordid greediness grasping at everything, not enduring to part with any thing, straining to unite advantages essentially incompatible. Goods are to be bought of foreigners, but the money which should pay for them is not to be exported in return. Capital is to be obtained from foreigners, in alternation of the waste produced by war loans, but the remuneration for it in the way of annuities, and the restitution of it, in the redemption of the annuities, is to be deplored and fought against as a grievance.

JEREMY BENTHAM
Defence of a Maxim, 1801

[81] The new wealth with which imperialism enriched Babylonia and Egypt was really just loot, and represented

no addition to the total supply of real wealth available to humanity; quite the contrary. The destruction of houses or the ravaging of gardens is the reverse of wealth-production. 'An army is a body of pure consumers, nay negative producers, producers of illth.' But money veils any discrepancy between real wealth, the available supply of commodities, and its consumption. Its possessors did not suffer from any shortage and could indeed make more money by loans to those who needed it to meet the rising prices.

GORDON CHILDE
What Happened in History, 1942

[82] Though it is in the power of human institutions to make everybody poor, they cannot make everybody rich.

NASSAU WILLIAM SENIOR
Journal, 1849

[83] The exchangeable value of all commodities rises as the difficulties of their production increase. If, then, new difficulties occur in the production of corn from more labour being necessary, whilst no more labour is required to produce gold, silver, cloth, linen, etc., the exchangeable value of corn will necessarily rise as compared with those things. . . . Wherever competition can have its full effect and the production of the commodity be not limited by nature, as is the case with some wines, the difficulty or facility of their production will ultimately regulate their exchangeable value.

DAVID RICARDO
On the Influence of a Low Price of Corn on the Profits of Stock, 1815

[84] It is true, it so happens by the appointment of Providence that valuable articles are in almost all instances obtained by Labour, but still this is an accidental, not an essential circumstance. If the aerolites which occasionally

fall were diamonds and pearls, and if these articles could be obtained in no other way, but were casually picked up, to the same amount as is now obtained by digging and diving, they would be of precisely the same value as now. In this, as in many other points in Political Economy, men are prone to confound cause and effect. It is not that pearls fetch a high price because men have dived for them; but, on the contrary, men dive for them because they fetch a high price.

RICHARD WHATELY
Introductory Lectures on Political Economy (3rd edn.), 1847

[85] The best and simplest general type of capital is a well-made ploughshare. . . . And the true home question, to every capitalist and to every nation, is not, 'How many ploughs have you?' but, 'where are your furrows?'

JOHN RUSKIN
'Ad Valorem', *Unto This Last*, 1862

[86] To admit that the criterion of commerce and industry is its success in discharging a social purpose is at once to turn property and economic activity from rights which are absolute into rights which are contingent and derivative, because it is to affirm that they are relative to functions and that they may be justly revoked when the functions are not performed. It is, in short, to imply that property and economic activity exist to promote the ends of society, whereas hitherto society has been regarded in the world of business as existing to promote them.

R. H. TAWNEY
The Acquisitive Society, 1921

[87] In the late war I knew a highly respected Member of Parliament of distinctly socialist opinions who sometimes lectured on elementary economics. He happened to be a corporal in the army, and instead of returning unused bread

to the stores, he was compelled by the public opinion of his company to bury it for fear their ration might be reduced.

In order to make the small economies which can be effected by single individuals belonging to the rank and file seem worth some inconvenience to themselves, the results must not be spread over a very wide area. The corporal's company did not mind wasting the bread, because the loss when spread over all the British taxpayers appeared very trifling to them compared with the possibility of their own ration being reduced to something less than what they might some time require.

EDWIN CANNAN
A Review of Economic Theory, 1929

[88] The mass of national profit must necessarily be composed of the sum total of individual profits: and the individual profits taken together must necessarily compose the mass of national profits. For me, an English merchant, it is by no means necessary, if I am to gain in my trade with a French merchant, that he should sustain a loss equal to my profit, or any loss whatsoever. His gain from what he receives from me is equal to my gain from what I receive from him. He is no more disposed to part with his goods at a loss than I am to part with mine at a disadvantage. We may, both of us, incur a loss, but that would be an accident no more characteristic of the ordinary course of trade than a shipwreck is characteristic of the ordinary course of navigation.

It is far from being the case that England has gained more from the other nations than the other nations from England: the opposite, in fact, is true. For in proportion as capital is more abundant, the rate of profit is less.

JEREMY BENTHAM
Of the Balance of Trade, 1801

[89] To divide men into two classes, productive and unproductive consumers, would in fact be a false division, there being few who do not in some respects belong to both classes. So far as a man's consumption is essential to his production, he belongs to the first class; so far as it is not essential, to the second. Those only can be called simply unproductive who return nothing whatever for what they consume; those only simply productive who indulge in no superfluous consumption whatever.

NASSAU WILLIAM SENIOR
An Outline of the Science of Political Economy, 1836

[90] Free competition is equivalent to a reward granted to those who furnish the best goods at the lowest prices. It offers an immediate and natural reward, which a crowd of rivals flatter themselves they shall obtain, and acts with greater efficacy than a distant punishment, from which each may hope to escape.

JEREMY BENTHAM
Principles of Penal Law, 1813

[91] At the historical dawn of capitalist production—and every capitalist upstart has personally to go through this historical stage—avarice and desire to get rich are the ruling passions. But the progress of capitalist production not only creates a world of delights; it lays open, in speculation and the credit system, a thousand sources of sudden enrichment. When a certain stage of development has been reached, a conventional degree of prodigality, which is also an exhibition of wealth and consequently a source of credit, becomes a business necessity to the 'unfortunate' capitalist. Luxury enters into capital's expenses of representation. Moreover, the capitalist gets rich, not like the miser in proportion to his personal labour and restricted consump-

tion, but at the same rate as he squeezes out the labour-power of others and enforces on the labourer abstinence from all life's enjoyments.

Although, therefore, the prodigality of the capitalist never possesses the bona-fide character of the open-handed feudal lord's prodigality, but on the contrary has always lurking behind it the most sordid avarice and the most anxious calculation, yet his expenditure grows with his accumulation, without the one necessarily restricting the other. But along with this growth, there is at the same time developed in his breast a Faustian conflict between the passion for accumulation, and the desire for enjoyment.

KARL MARX
Capital, 1867

[92] In the case of most men the only inducement which has been found sufficiently constant and unflagging to overcome the ever-present influence of indolence and love of ease, and induce men to apply themselves unrelaxingly to work for the most part in itself dull and unexciting, is the prospect of bettering their own economic condition and that of their family.

JOHN STUART MILL
Chapters on Socialism, 1897 (posthumous)

[93] The right to use a piece of land gives command over a certain space—a certain part of the earth's surface. The area of the earth is fixed; the geometric relations in which any part of its stands to other parts are fixed. Man has no control over them; they are wholly unaffected by demand; they have no cost of production; there is no supply price at which they can be produced. The use of a certain area of the earth's surface is a primary condition of anything that man can do; it gives him room for his own action, with the

enjoyment of the heat and light, the air and the rain which nature assigns to that area; and it determines his distance from, and in a great measure his relation to, other things and other persons. ALFRED MARSHALL

Principles of Economics, 1890

[94] It is evident that if the incomes of the rich were taken from them and divided among the poor as we stand at present, the poor would be very little less poor; the supply of capital would cease because nobody could afford to save; the country houses would fall into ruins; and learning and science and art and literature and all the rest of what we call culture would perish. BERNARD SHAW

The Intelligent Woman's Guide to Socialism and Capitalism, 1928

[95] The element of profit . . . is the mainspring of the expansion of employment in all countries of the world except Russia. Everything that touches that element of profit has an important effect on the whole community. It is not merely a question of social justice. Anything which makes it more difficult to bring together these elements has an effect on the speed and the mechanism and the adjustment of the machine which provides employment.

SIR JOSIAH STAMP

In *The World's Economic Crisis*, 1932

[96] Mrs Nosnibor went on to say that I must not think there was any want of confidence in the bank because I had seen so few people there; the heart of the country was thoroughly devoted to these establishments, and any sign of their being in danger would bring in support from the most unexpected quarters. It was only because people knew them to be so very safe that in some cases (as she lamented to say in Mr Nos-

nibor's) they felt that their support was unnecessary. Moreover, these institutions never departed from the safest and most approved banking principles. Thus they never allowed interest on deposit, a thing now frequently done by certain bubble companies, which by doing an illegitimate trade had drawn many customers away; and even the shareholders were fewer than formerly, owing to the innovations of these unscrupulous persons, for the Musical Banks paid little or no dividend but divided their profits by way of bonus on the original shares once in every thirty thousand years; and as it was now only two thousand years since there had been one of these distributions, people felt that they could not hope for another in their own time and preferred investments whereby they got some more tangible return; all which, she said was very melancholy to think of.

SAMUEL BUTLER
Erewhon, 1872

[97] It is affluence that creates poverty, as it is the public that creates privacy. In a tribal society there is neither privacy nor poverty. When everybody starves at the same rate, there is no poverty.

MARSHALL MCLUHAN
McLuhan Dew-Line Newsletter, 1969

[98] It is unsound to assume that wealth is the *cause* of poverty. That is, we hold, one of the popular delusions of our time. The position to which our studies in this book bring us, is that both irresponsible wealth and poverty are produced by a faulty, inaccurate economic mechanism, as smoke, noise, dirt and delay are produced by a badly adjusted motor-car.

H. G. WELLS
The Work, Wealth and Happiness of Mankind, 1932

[99] It is too hastily believed that the poor are poor because the rich have taken something away from them. . . . Certainly the machine gives here and deprives there. But that is not by any means the same thing as taking from one and giving to another. It is not a process that can be remedied by selling up the rich man and giving all that he has to the poor.

H. G. WELLS
The Work, Wealth and Happiness of Mankind, 1932

[100] When we talk of poverty in the midst of plenty we should always remember that we mean *relative* plenty. Absolutely, the maximum utilization of the world's productive equipment would still leave us, on the average, very badly off.

LIONEL ROBBINS
'The Twofold Roots of the Great Depression', in *The Burden of Plenty?*, 1935

[101] Increased means and increased leisure are the two civilizers of man.

BENJAMIN DISRAELI
Speech to the Conservatives of Manchester, 1873

[102] This is not a crisis of poverty but a crisis of abundance. It is not the harshness and the niggardliness of nature which is oppressing us, but our own incompetence and wrong-headedness which hinders us from making use of the bountifulness of inventive science and causes us to be overwhelmed by its generous fruits. The voices which—in such a conjuncture—tell us that the path of escape is to be found in strict economy and in refraining, wherever possible, from utilizing the world's potential production, are the voices of fools and madmen.

JOHN MAYNARD KEYNES
In *The World's Economic Crisis*, 1932

[103] Both rich and poor are really hateful in themselves. For

my part I hate the poor and look forward eagerly to their extermination. I pity the rich a little, but am equally bent on their extermination. BERNARD SHAW
The Intelligent Woman's Guide to Socialism and Capitalism, 1928

[104] Things are valuable, in terms of money, in proportion as they are scarce.

The object of Capitalism is not to make as many things as possible, but as much value as possible.

Therefore Capitalism aims at scarcity. G. D. H. COLE
Economic Tracts for the Times, 1932

[105] Real value consists in the power of a thing to satisfy human needs and desires, irrespective of the power of those who have the needs or desires to pay for it. G. D. H. COLE
Economic Tracts for The Times, 1932

[106] Some people imagine that because they can save money the wealth of the world can be stored up. Stuff and nonsense. Most of the wealth that keeps us alive will not last a week. The world lives from hand to mouth. BERNARD SHAW
The Intelligent Woman's Guide to Socialism and Capitalism, 1928

[107] What is meant by bounteousness without any cost? Follow what is the profit of the people, and profit them; is this not bounteousness without any cost? CONFUCIUS
c. 490 B.C.

[108] The supreme power cannot take from any man part of his property without his own consent: for the preservation of property being the end of government, and that for which man enter into society, it necessarily supposes and requires that the people should have property, without which

they must be supposed to lose that, by entering into society, which was the end for which they entered into it; too gross an absurdity for any man to own. JOHN LOCKE

The Second Treatise of Civil Government, 1690

[109] There is a great principle for the increase of wealth: those who produce it should be many; those who consume it, few. Those who create it should be rapid; and those who use it, slow. Then wealth will always be sufficient.

CONFUCIUS

C. 490 B.C.

[110] Men nearly always speak and write as if riches were absolute, and it were possible, by following certain scientific precepts, for everybody to be rich. Whereas riches are a power like that of electricity, acting only through inequalities or negations of itself. The force of the guinea you have in your pocket depends wholly on the default of a guinea in your neighbours' pocket. If he did not want it, it would be of no use to you; the degree of power it possesses depends accurately upon the need or desire he has for it—and the art of making yourself rich, in the ordinary mercantile economist's sense, is therefore equally and necessarily the art of keeping your neighbour poor. JOHN RUSKIN

'The Veins of Wealth', *Unto This Last*, 1862

[111] The bulk of our poor are poor because they produce the wrong things. What then are the right ones? Trade is always working at this problem solving it ill or well as our traders are wise or foolish.

The question whether one man really could under a system of pure barter be rich at the expense of his neighbour is altogether of secondary importance and greatly a matter of words. The man who produced much would be rich, but his produce would be enjoyed by all who gave him what they valued less. Nevertheless, if by producing much he threw others out of work, he might be said to be rich at their expense; but this would be a very unfair way to word it, since when they found out new right things to make, they would all be rich and be richer than before. It is absolutely false to suppose that the well-being of one man must entail the ill-being of another, but it may produce it.

FLEEMING JENKIN
Essays on Political Economy, 1887

[112] An economy campaign, in my opinion, is a beggar-my-neighbour enterprise. just as much as competitive tariffs or competitive wage-reductions, which are perhaps more obviously of this description. For one man's expenditure is another man's income.

JOHN MAYNARD KEYNES
In *The World's Economic Crisis*, 1932

[113] Let inventive men consider whether the secret of this universe does after all consist in making money. With a hell which means 'failing to make money' I do not think there is any heaven possible that would suit one well. In brief, all this Mammon gospel of supply-and-demand, competition, *laissez faire*, and devil take the hindmost begins to be one of the shabbiest gospels ever preached.

THOMAS CARLYLE
Past and Present, 1843

[114] From time immemorial the better sort have agreed that a race of well-to-do brutes, without mind or emotions,

lacking a sense of spiritual values—amongst which stands pre-eminently a sense of freedom—would be entirely worthless. Yet the economic argument, shrewdly urged on employers of labour, is said to have been the one that carried most weight in the American prohibition campaign. If that be so, it means that the greatest country in whose hands, some think, lies the fate of the world, shamelessly sold freedom for cash; for cash it made law contemptible, and for cash was content to make itself ridiculous. CLIVE BELL

On British Freedom, 1923

[115] Is the possession or preservation of capital the end, or the means? The means, undoubtedly, What we want is an abundance of commodities, and if it could be proved that, by the sacrifice of a part of our capital, we should augment the annual produce of those objects which contribute to our enjoyment and happiness, we ought not, I should think, to repine at the loss of a part of our capital. DAVID RICARDO

On Protection to Agriculture, 1822

[116] No economist would admit national economy to be legitimate which proposed to itself only the building of a pyramid of gold. He would declare the gold to be wasted, were it to remain in the monumental form, and would say it ought to be employed. But to what end? Either it must be used only to gain more gold, and build a larger pyramid, or for some purpose other than the gaining of gold. And this other purpose, however at first apprehended, will be found to resolve itself finally into the service of Man—that is to say, the extension, defence or comfort of his life. The golden pyramid may perhaps be providently built, perhaps improvidently; but the wisdom or folly of the accumulation

can only be determined by our having first clearly stated the aim of all economy, namely, the extension of life.

JOHN RUSKIN
Munera Pulveris, 1880

[117] The capitalist is as likely, perhaps, to be in want as the labourer. It is true that the distress of the labourer us much more conspicuous, and that he advertises it; he goes about saying, 'I am starving, and it is the tyranny of capital which is killing me.' But it is also true that the capitalist is in danger of ruin, and that he conceals it. If he cannot complete contracts which he has made, if he has to stay out of a return from his business longer than he can afford, he is ruined. But he will never say this, because it may injure his credit and quicken the coming of the evil.

WALTER BAGEHOT
Economic Studies, 1888

[118] It must be admitted that 'self-denial' and 'self-help' would make a poor rallying cry for the hustings; and it is to be feared that the patriotism of this day has but little regard for such common things as individual economy and providence, although it is by the practice of such virtues only that the genuine independence of the industrial classes is to be secured.

SAMUEL SMILES
Self-Help, 1858

[119] From the point of view of expediency it is surely clear that a system which guaranteed the same reward to the industrious and to the idle, to the clever and to the stupid, would be a system which would be very much less productive than, in our present state of comparative poverty, any sensible person would regard as satisfactory. I am not in the

least arguing that the pecuniary incentive is the only incentive; I am not denying that scientists and social reformers and others whose product is of great importance do much without much regard to financial reward. But I am arguing that the great majority of jobs have not such intrinsic interest and that you cannot assume that the workaday business of the world will get done very well without some connection, direct or indirect, between effort and reward. I think that the experience of the Russian experiment shows that this is at least as true of collectivist societies as it is of societies based on private property and the market. LORD ROBBINS

'Equality as a Social Objective', *Politics and Economics*, 1961

[120] There are valuable human activities which require the motive of money-making and the environment of private wealth-ownership for their full fruition.

. . . Dangerous human proclivities can be canalized into comparatively harmless channels by the existence of opportunities for money-making and private wealth, which, if they cannot be satisfied in this way, may find their outlet in cruelty, the reckless pursuit of personal power and authority, and other forms of self-aggrandisement.

It is better that a man should tyrannize over his bank balance than over his fellow-citizens.

JOHN MAYNARD KEYNES

The General Theory of Employment, Interest and Money, 1936

[121] Every body of men is governed altogether by its conception of what is its interest, in the narrowest and most selfish sense of the word interest: never by any regard for the interest of the people. In that position, none of those inducements, any one of which may suffice to cause a single man to make sacrifice of his private interest to the universal

interest, can have place: viz. desire of reputation, pleasure of sympathy for the people, pleasure of power in respect of the secret consciousness of having had so large a share in contributing to the happiness of the people. Yes, perhaps for a moment, under an excitation produced by a fine speech: but for anything of a continuance, never is any body of men determined by any other consideration than its conception of what is in the highest degree beneficial to its purely self-regarding interests. JEREMY BENTHAM

The Psychology of Economic Man, c. 1799

[122] A whole school of cheerful optimism has been based upon the creed that if every man pursues his own interests in an enlightened manner we shall get the best of possible results, because it will be to his interest to apply his energies where they are 'most useful to others'. Yes, but what others? The answer is, 'those who already have most of everything else that they want'. This automatic action of the economic forces is at the service of every man exactly in inverse proportion to the urgency of his wants. The very fact that he is in want of everything prevents his giving much for anything, and makes his command of the economic forces light. The very fact that he has abundance of all things enables him to give largely of valued things for the gratification of the slightest impulse, for he is only checking impulses equally slight. The weight that his passing whim can throw into the economic scale is heavier than that which can throw into the economic scale is heavier than that which his neighbour can pit against it to save his life. The gospel of economic optimism, in a word, is the gospel, 'to him that hath shall be given'. PHILIP H. WICKSTEED

The Common Sense of Political Economy, 1910

[123] Let us clear from the ground the metaphysical or general principles upon which, from time to time, *laissez-faire* has been founded. It is *not* true that individuals possess a prescriptive 'natural liberty' in their economic activities. There is *no* 'compact' conferring perpetual rights on those who Have or on those who Acquire. The world is *not* so governed from above that private and social interest always coincide. It is *not* so managed here below that in practice they coincide. It is *not* a correct deduction from the Principles of Economics that enlightened self-interest always operates in the public interest. Nor is it true that self-interest generally *is* enlightened; more often individuals acting separately to promote their own ends are too ignorant or too weak to attain even these. Experience does *not* show that individuals, when they make up a social unit, are always less clear-sighted than when they act separately.

We cannot, therefore, settle on abstract grounds, but must handle on its merits in detail, what Burke termed 'one of the finest problems in legislation, namely, to determine what the State ought to take upon itself to direct by the public wisdom, and what it ought to leave, with as little interference as possible, to individual exertions.'

JOHN MAYNARD KEYNES
Essays in Persuasion, 1931

[124] The laws of demand and supply, rigid as they are, point to no necessary impoverishment and degradation of the labourer as men and means multiply. . . . Convince these paupers of their own misery. Teach them what comfort is, and a rational self-interest will lead them to indpendence, which the more wealthy have reached by the same path. Rational self-interest has done most things in this world,

the great duty of the teacher being to distinguish rational from irrational self-interest. Whatever school of religion or philosophy we belong to, we cannot deny that each man, acting rationally for his own advantage, will conduce to the good of all; and if the motive be not the highest, it is one which at least can always be counted on.

FLEEMING JENKIN
Essays on Political Economy, 1887

[125] The lower classes . . . grossly miscalculate the number and value of the prizes in the lottery of life: they think that they have drawn little better than blanks, and believe those who tell them that if all the high lots were abolished everybody might have a hundred-pound note.

NASSAU WILLIAM SENIOR
Journal, 1849

[126] What the worker needs, if you would keep him working, is plainly a check for 'anything money can buy' in return for his services rendered. Our modern economic organization, our whole modern human society, has grown upon the assumption, the colourable pretence at least, that the money distributed in wages does give that, and I cannot conceive of it carrying on now in any other fashion without becoming unrecognizably different. Our civilization can as little give up the use of money now, as our bodies can the use of blood. The practical problem is to ensure the best blood possible—to keep out poisons and contagions and avoid anaemia.

H. G. WELLS
The Work, Wealth and Happiness of Mankind, 1932

[127] A native of the United States clings to this world's goods as if he were certain never to die; and he is so hasty

in grasping at all within his reach that one would suppose he was constantly afraid of not living long enough to enjoy them. He clutches everything, he holds nothing fast, but soon loosens his grasp to pursue fresh gratifications.

In the United States a man builds a house to spend his later years in it, and he sells it before the roof is on; he plants a garden and lets it just when the trees are beginning to bear; he brings a field into cultivation and leaves other men to gather the crops. He embraces a profession and gives it up. He settles in a place, which he soon afterward leaves, to carry his changeable lodgings elsewhere. . . . Death at length overtakes him, but it is before he is weary of the futile chase of that complete happiness which is forever on the wing.

ALEXIS DE TOCQUEVILLE
Democracy in America, 1835

[128] A man is rich or poor, according to the abundance of necessaries and luxuries which he can command; and whether the exchangeable value of these for money, for corn, or for labour, be high or low, they will equally contribute to the enjoyment of their possessor. It is through confounding the ideas of value and wealth, or riches that it has been asserted, that by diminishing the quantity of commodities, that is to say of the necessaries, conveniences, and enjoyments of human life, riches may be increased. If value were the measure of riches, this could not be denied, because by scarcity the value of commodities is raised; but if Adam Smith be correct, if riches consist in necessaries and enjoyments, then they cannot be increased by a diminution of quantity.

It is true, that the man in possession of a scarce commodity is richer, if by means of it he can command more of the necessaries and enjoyments of human life; but as the general stock out of which each man's riches are drawn, is diminished in quantity, by all that any individual takes from it, other men's shares must necessarily be reduced in proportion as this favoured individual is able to appropriate a greater quantity to himself. DAVID RICARDO

The Principles of Political Economy and Taxation, 1817

[129] The business motive is a good servant but a bad master, and a society which gives itself up to the dominance of the business motive is a bad society. We do not put first things first in putting ourselves first. In former days there was a great alternative to the pursuit of gain, as the guiding force in society; there was force for good inspired by religious belief and based on membership of a Christian community. Now this religious force for good is less widely influential than it was in the nineteenth century. It must either be revived or be replaced by some equally good alternative, if that can be found. Perhaps it must be both in part revived and in part replaced. LORD BEVERIDGE

Voluntary Action: a Report on Methods of Social Advance, 1948

[130] The nineteenth century in Britain was a time of private enterprise, not only in pursuit of gain, but also in social reform. The interplay of these two motives of gain and service in the fields covered by this survey is one of its themes. In the nineteenth century many men made fortunes for themselves in meeting the needs of their fellows. Many others, driven by social conscience to attack want, squalor, ignorance, disease and idleness, inspired or created societies and institutions to serve their aims. The amount of unhappiness that has been put out of the world through the lives and works of such men as Lord Shaftesbury

with his Ragged School Union, or Elizabeth Fry with her attack on cruel stupidity in the prisons, or Charles Booth the originator of Social Surveys, or Samuel Barnett, the founder of Toynbee Hall, or Benjamin Waugh the founder of the National Society for the Prevention of Cruelty to Children, is beyond all calculation. LORD BEVERIDGE

Voluntary Action, a Report on Methods of Social Advance, 1948

[131] In truth, there is no such thing as a growth industry, I believe. There are only companies organized and operated to create and capitalize on growth opportunities. Industries that assume themselves to be riding some automatic growth escalator invariably descend into stagnation. The history of every dead and dying 'growth' industry shows a self-deceiving cycle of bountiful expansion and undetected decay.

THEODORE LEVITT

'Marketing Myopia', *Harvard Business Review*, 1960

[132] We are so used to thinking primarily in terms of the battle for profit and advancement that we find it difficult to conceive of another kind of world. But let us remember that if real economic security is assured through State social services, the world will look very different to many struggling wage-earners. Then, as planning increases in scale and in efficiency, it will remove much of the instability and risk which now besets business enterprise. And a lessening of risk means a lowering of the rate of return on investment. JULIAN HUXLEY

Democracy Marches, 1941

[133] Some evil genius invented the term profit motive and started the notion that private enterprise is a scramble for profit to the exclusion of all the other considerations

that govern trade. Here is one of those half-truths which are much more dangerous than the direct lie, and it is pathetic that a great many people engaged in business are themselves unaware that the profit they seek is no more than a measure or gauge by which to know whether all their efforts to make, import export, sell and generally carry on, are good or bad. SIR ERNEST BENN

The State the Enemy, 1953

[134] It is unfortunate that in recent years the word 'profits' has come to have in the minds of many people an evil connotation. The pressure of public opinion on the concept of profits has become so intense that some companies have even succumbed to the temptation of trying to pretend that they do not exist by calling them something else. 'Margins', 'available balances for dividends and reinvestment', and such like euphemisms are a sign of how deeply this canker has eaten into the proper respect that the public at large should have for industrial effort. The image of a shareholder in the public mind is invariably that of a fat man in a black coat and striped trousers smoking a big cigar as he glides towards his city office in his Rolls-Royce. The facts are so ludicrously different from this that it is difficult to see how such a picture has been allowed to develop. But although there are millions of shareholders in this country who have only very small holdings—albeit often representing a major portion of their income—only when the holding of shares becomes common among all wage-earners will the profit motive in business become respectable again. Until this happens, the government of the day, of whatever political complexion, will feel that it has a free hunting licence to go after the profits of enterprise. D. H. BARRAN

'Incentives and Growth', in *Growth Through Industry*, 1967

[135] A decent provision for the poor is the true test of civilization.

SAMUEL JOHNSON
Boswell's *Life*, 1770

[136] The rule is, jam tomorrow, and jam yesterday—but never jam today.

LEWIS CARROLL
Alice Through the Looking-Glass, 1872

[137] The dark shadow of the Malthusian philosophy has passed away, and no view of the ultimate scheme of things would now be accepted under which multitudes of men and women are doomed by inevitable law to a struggle for existence so severe as necessarily to cripple or destroy the higher parts of their nature.

E. SEEBOHM ROWNTREE
Poverty: a Study of Town Life, 1900

[138] It is good enough to talk of God whilst we are sitting here after a nice breakfast and looking forward to a nicer luncheon, but how am I to talk of God to the millions who have to go without two meals a day? To them God can only appear to be bread.

MAHATMA GANDHI
1869–1948

[139] 'I saw Manning and his wife hung. Mrs Manning was dressed beautiful when she came up. She screeched when Jack Ketch pulled the bolt away. . . . I did 4s. 6d. at the hanging—two handkerchiefs, and a purse with 2s. in it. . . . But a shilling honest goes further than 5s. stolen. Some call that only a saying, but it's true.'

A young pickpocket,
quoted by Henry Mayhew, *London Labour and the London Poor*, 1861–62

[140] However willing the working classes may be to remain in passive opposition merely to the existing social system,

they will not continue to bear, they cannot, the awful uncertainties of their lives. Minimum standards of wages and comfort, insurance in some effective form against sickness, unemployment, old age—these are the questions, and the only questions, by which parties are going to live in future. WINSTON CHURCHILL
1874–1965

[141] You should not think of social service purely as State action, not only as the wonderful voluntary work which is being done. . . . We must realize that the amenities of life, like its essentials, are best secured by the personal effort and individual contribution of every member of the community, and are not a sort of heaven-sent manna to be garnered and enjoyed without effort, service, or obligation.
H.R.H. THE PRINCE OF WALES
27 January, 1931

[142] Poverty: you don't need experts from the universities or the City of London to tell you what that is. The experts on poverty are the poor themselves. HUGH DALTON
'Our Present Discontents', in *The Burden of Plenty?*, 1935

[143] To those people in the huts and villages of half the globe struggling to break the bounds of mass misery, we pledge our best efforts to help them help themselves, for whatever period is required—not because the communists may be doing it, not because we seek their votes, but because it is right. JOHN F. KENNEDY
Inaugural Presidential Address, 20 January, 1961

[144] If the rich nations made a determined move to shape their general economic policies more in the interests of the

under-developed ones, this would be of a vastly greater consequence to the economic development of those countries than any aid which they could ever hope to get. If instead the rich countries persist in carrying on their ordinary business with the under-developed world on the principle of narrow economic nationalism and adjustments to the wishes of short-sighted vested interests at home, even generous aid becomes nothing more than a palliative.

GUNNER MYRDAL
Beyond the Welfare State, 1960

[145] The type of relationship which the industrialized countries are setting up with the young and poor nations . . . threatens to warp their mentality. Without reviving old-fashioned paternalist ideas, one is entitled to say that the most-developed countries have a moral responsibility towards the under-developed ones, which are passing through a kind of adolescence not only in the economic sphere but also, at least in many cases, mentally as well. And all too often the way in which aid is given might well lead them secretly to despise the donor, whether justifiably or not. For they see that aid is not necessarily given to the country which can show that it is making personal efforts to further its own growth, or that the aid received will form part of a sound plan of development. They see that other and less logical arguments are more compelling. The arts of innuendo can be employed to hint that one is tempted to yield to advances from another quarter and this does not foster an atmosphere of integrity.

The young and poor nations are in danger of entering upon the stage of history with the mental paraphernalia of prostitutes, and the Big Powers are to blame for this.

PIERRE MOUSSA
The Under-Privileged Nations, 1962

III

Functions of Money

[146] Now what money does for us is to act as a sort of pledge or guarantee that a prospective exchange of commodities will in fact take place if the necessity arises, though in the meantime the necessity is not immediate. For if we proffer the money it should be possible for us to get the goods. No doubt money is subject to the vagaries of the market just like other commodities, for its purchasing power keeps rising and falling. Still, it is pretty constant. For this reason everything should be rated at a fixed value in money, for that will always make exchange possible and, if exchange, association for the purpose of exchange. So money acts as a measure which, by making things commensurable, renders it possible to make them equal. Without exchange there could be no association, without equality there could be no exchange, without commensurability there could be no equality. Strictly speaking no doubt things so widely different can never become commensurable. Still in demand we have a common measure which will be found to work pretty well. Some one standard there must be, and it must be accepted by a general agreement or understanding. Such a standard has the effect of making all things commensurable, since they can all be measured by money. Suppose A is a house, B ten pounds, C a bed. Then (supposing the house to be worth five pounds and a bed one) $A = B/2$ and $C = B/10$ Now we see how many beds are equal to a house, namely, five. It is obvious that in times when money did not yet exist exchange must have been effected on this principle. For—putting convenience on one side—it makes no difference whether you pay five beds for a house or the value of five beds.

ARISTOTLE
The *Ethics*, Book V, c. 335 B.C.

[147] [Money is] the sanguification of the commonwealth . . . and circulating nourisheth by the way every member of the body.

THOMAS HOBBES
The *Leviathan*, 1651

[148] 'No man of religion or other shall henceforth carry the sterling out of the realm of England, nor silver in plate, nor vessels of gold or silver, on pain of forfeiture of the money, plate or vessels that he shall carry, without special licence from us.'

EDWARD III
In an ordnance, 1336

[149] All things are dearer under a bad government, and cheaper under a good one.

REV. SYDNEY SMITH
1831

[150] Money is not, properly speaking, one of the subjects of commerce; but only the instrument which men have agreed upon to facilitate the exchange of one commodity for another. It is none of the wheels of trade: it is the oil which renders the motion of the wheels more smooth and easy.

DAVID HUME
Of Money, 1752

[151] Money has been inaccurately spoken of as merely a means of exchange. But it is far more than this. It is a documentary expression of legal claim. It is not wealth, but a documentary claim to wealth, being the sign of the relative quantities of it, or of the labour producing it, to which, at a given time, persons, or societies, are entitled.

If all the money in the world, notes and gold, were destroyed in an instant, it would leave the world neither richer nor poorer than it was. But it would leave the individual inhabitants of it in different relations.

JOHN RUSKIN
Munera Pulveris, 1880

[152] Money is one of the most fundamental of all Man's inventions. Every branch of knowledge has its fundamental discovery. In mechanics it is the wheel, in science fire, in politics the vote. Similarly, in economics, in the whole commercial side of Man's social existence, money is the essential invention on which all the rest is based.

GEOFFREY CROWTHER
An Outline of Money, 1948

[153] Money . . . enables us to get what we want instead of what other people think we want. BERNARD SHAW
The Intelligent Woman's Guide to Socialism and Capitalism, 1928

[154] By Annual Income we mean the whole that arises in any Country from Lands and its Product, from Foreign Trade and Domestick Business, as Arts, Manufactures, etc. And by Annual Expence we understand what is of necessity consum'd to Cloath and Feed the People, or what is requisite for their Defence in time of War or for their Ornament in time of Peace. And where the Annual Income exceeds the Expence, there is a Superlucration arising, which may be called Wealth or National Stock.

DR CHARLES DAVENANT
Natural and Political Observations and Conclusions upon the State and Condition of England, 1696

[155] Money . . . the great wheel of circulation, the great instrument of commerce, like all other instruments of trade,

though it makes a part and a very valuable part of the capital, makes no part of the revenue of the society to which it belongs; and though the metal pieces of which it is composed, in the course of their annual circulation, distribute to every man the revenue which properly belongs to him, they make themselves no part of that revenue. ADAM SMITH

The Wealth of Nations, 1776

[156] If, from increasing opulence, more commodities came to be bought and sold, the first effect would be that the value of money would rise. . . . This profit, however, could not long continue; for the quantity of money which, by these means, would be added to the circulation, would sink its value, whilst the diminishing quantity of bullion in the market would tend also to raise the value of bullion to that of coin; from one or both these causes a perfect equality in their value could not fail to be soon restored.

DAVID RICARDO

Proposals for an Economical and Secure Currency, 1816

[157] Money is one of the greatest of human inventions, comparable to the wheel or the steam engine. Its rise was contemporary with that of civilization itself. In periods when it went out of favour, such as the age of high feudalism, the mass of people were in a condition literally of serfdom, and the arts and sciences and civilization itself were stagnant. And we ought therefore to view with alarm the modern tendency to displace money by fixed prices, import programmes, bilateral commercial agreement, hard and soft currencies, etc. It is sometimes said that the social sciences are not keeping pace with the physical sciences. But here is a symptom of an actual deterioration in our social arrangements. . . .

Voices have indeed been raised, by reaction to the prevailing trend, in favour of a free pricing system as safeguarding the consumer's liberty of choice. Money is represented as a bulwark of liberty, as indeed it is. Poor and depressed as the working classes of this country were a hundred years ago—Socialists are apt to say that freedom of choice is only valued by the rich—they instinctively rebelled against the 'truck' system by which rations instead of freely usable money were supplied by employers. The 'truck' system, which is what we now have, is not so much better for being arranged by a democratic Government. But it is not only as a bulwark of liberty that money should be valued, but also as an instrument of efficiency. It is money that ensures the smooth working of our highly complicated productivity processes. ROY HARROD

Are These Hardships Necessary?, 1947

[158] Man is of all pieces of luggage the most difficult to be removed. In general an ill-paid labourer early in life gives hostages to misfortune, he burdens himself with the support of a wife and children; he cannot move, or they would starve. But civilization has invented an elaborate machinery for holding capital in a transferable form. The basis of this machinery is the invention of money.

WALTER BAGEHOT

Economic Studies, 1879

[159] Credit is believability. Because the economic system is in a state of productive expansion, we believe we will be repaid our debts tomorrow. Once a large number of people believe in this productive expansion of the economy, then the domestic economy almost unconsciously switches from supposedly immutable gold to intangible promises to pay,

to cheques, diners' cards and finally perhaps to the domestic computer in which you merely state your own index number or press your own button in order to record your purchases and financial obligations. It is the believability of the conviction that all debts will be paid which is the foundation of the system. That is why it is called a 'credit' economy.

BARBARA WARD
Poverty and Politics, 1969

[160] The wealth of a Country will depend on the question, whether the tastes of its inhabitants lead them to prefer objects of slow or rapid destruction.

NASSAU WILLIAM SENIOR
An Outline of the Science of Political Economy, 1836

[161] If we command our wealth, we shall be rich and free; if our wealth commands us, we are poor indeed.

EDMUND BURKE
Letters on a Regicide Peace, 1796

[162] The price of a commodity may rise while its value falls, and vice versa. A hat may rise from twenty to thirty shillings in price, but thirty shillings may not procure so much tea, sugar, coffee, and all other things, as twenty shillings did before, consequently a hat cannot procure so much. The hat, then, has fallen in value, though it has increased in price.

DAVID RICARDO
Proposals for an Economical and Secure Currency, 1816

[163] On the subject of the right employment of wealth, Johnson observed, 'A man cannot make bad use of his money, so far as regards Society, if he does not hoard it; for if he either spends it or lends it out, Society has the benefit.

It is in general better to spend money than to give it away; for industry is more promoted by spending money than by giving it away. A man who spends his money is sure he is doing good with it: he is not so sure when he gives it away. A man who spends ten thousand a year will do more good than a man who spends two thousand and gives away eight.'

JAMES BOSWELL
Life of Johnson, 1793

[164] A nation is rich, not according to the abundance of its money, not to the high value at which its commodities circulate, but according to the abundance of its commodities, contributing to its comforts and enjoyments. Although this is a proposition from which few would dissent, many look with the greatest alarm at the prospect of the diminution of their money revenue, though such reduced revenue should have so improved in exchangeable value as to procure considerably more of all the necessaries and luxuries of life.

DAVID RICARDO
Influence of a Low Price of Corn on the Profits of Stock, 1815

[165] Capital is most advantageously employed when no inducement whatsoever is made use of to turn it out of one employment into another. It is most advantageously employed when it follows that direction which the interest of the owners would, of its own accord, impress upon it.

JOHN STUART MILL
Elements of Political Economy, 1848

[166] Capital must be propelled by self-interest; it cannot be enticed by benevolence.

WALTER BAGEHOT
Economic Studies, 1879

[167] The principal way in which capital increases in England now, is by abstinence from enjoyment. We receive our incomes in money, and either we spend them on our enjoyments, in which case capital is not increased, for our incomes are all gone and no new productive thing is made, or we abstain from enjoyment and put our money into trade ourselves, supposing that we are in trade, and supposing that we are not in trade, lend it to those who are. The productive part of wealth—the wealth which creates other wealth—is augmented mainly by our not enjoying our incomes.

WALTER BAGEHOT
Economic Studies, 1888

[168] The influence of history, a mighty Empire, a cosmopolitan Stock Exchange, intimate business connections throughout the world, cheap money, a free gold market, steady exchanges, an almost unlimited market for capital, an elastic system of company legislation, a model insurance organization . . . these are the factors which have created Britain's financial supremacy.

Article in *Frankfürter Zeitung*, 1914

[169] A monetary economy . . . is essentially one in which changing views about the future are capable of influencing the quantity of employment and not merely its direction. But our method of analysing the economic behaviour of the present under the influence of changing ideas about the future is one which depends on the interaction of supply and demand, and is in this way linked up with our fundamental theory of value. JOHN MAYNARD KEYNES
Preface to *The General Theory of Employment, Interest and Money*, 1936

[170] We are, I think, a slow-moving race. Looking back

over the post-war period, it is almost incredible how long it has taken the owners of money to wake up to what has been going on. Even today . . . our investment mentality is utterly different from that of investors on the Continent. Yet because of the enormous weight of monetary debt in Britain —a weight untouched by currency purges, little reduced (in Continental terms) by the relatively slight inflation we have had, constantly added to by profligate governments—we are terribly vulnerable to any flight from money and money stocks. HAROLD WINCOTT
'Keynes Up to Date', *The Business of Capitalism*, 1968

[171] It is also evident, that the prices do not so much depend on the absolute quantity of commodities and that of money, which are in a nation, as on that of the commodities, which come or may come to market, and of the money which circulates. If the coin be locked up in chests, it is the same thing with regard to prices, as if it were annihilated; if the commodities be hoarded in magazines and granaries, a like effect follows. As the money and commodities, in these cases, never meet, they cannot affect each other. Were we, at any time, to form conjectures concerning the price of provisions, the corn, which the farmer must reserve for seed and for the maintenance of himself and family, ought never to enter into the estimation. It is only the overplus, compared to the demand, that determines the value. DAVID HUME
Of Money, 1752

[172] If I, having a crown in my pocket, and not being athirst, hesitate whether I should buy a bottle of claret with it for my own drinking, or lay it out in providing for a family I see about to perish for want of any assistance, so

much the worse for me at the long run; but it is plain that, so long as I continue hesitating, the two pleasures of sensuality in the one case, of sympathy in the other, were exactly worth to me five shillings, to me they were exactly equal.

I beg a truce here of our man of sentiment and feeling while from necessity, and it is only from necessity, I speak and prompt mankind to speak a mercenary language. The Thermometer is the instrument for measuring the heat of the weather: the Barometer the instrument for measuring the pressure of the Air. Those who are not satisfied with the accuracy of those instruments must find out others that shall be more accurate, or bid adieu to Natural Philosophy. Money is the instrument of measuring the quantity of pain or pleasure. Those who are not satisfied with the accuracy of this instrument must find out some other that shall be more accurate, or bid adieu to politics and morals.

JEREMY BENTHAM
The Philosophy of Economic Science, 1793

[173] There is no subtler, no surer means of overturning the existing basis of society than to debauch the currency. The process engages all the hidden forces of economic law on the side of destruction, and does it in a manner which not one man in a million is able to diagnose.

JOHN MAYNARD KEYNES
The Economic Consequences of the Peace, 1919

[174] Unless a plan of finance is of the nature of a commercial undertaking, it cannot give to Government more than it takes away, either from individuals or from Government itself, under some other form. Something cannot be made out of nothing, by the stroke of a wand. In whatever way an

operation may be disguised, whatever forms we may constrain a value to take, whatever metamorphosis we may make it undergo, we can only have a value by creating it, or by taking it from others. The very best of all plans of finance is to spend little, and the best of all taxes is that which is the least in amount. JEAN BAPTISTE SAY

Traité d'Economique Politique, 1803

[175] Taxation can never be so equally applied, as to operate in the same proportion on the value of all commodities, and still to preserve them at the same relative value. It frequently operates very differently from the intention of the legislature, by its indirect effects. DAVID RICARDO

The Principles of Political Economy and Taxation, 1821 (3rd edn.)

[176] The best taxes are such as levied upon consumptions, especially those of luxury; because such taxes are least felt by the people. They seem, in some measure, voluntary; since a man may chuse how far he will use the commodity which is taxed: They are paid gradually, and insensibly: They naturally produce sobriety and frugality, if judiciously imposed: And being confounded with the natural price of the commodity, they are scarcely perceived by the consumers. Their only disadvantage is, that they are expensive in the levying.

Taxes upon possessions are levied without expence; but have every other disadvantage. Most states, however, are obliged to have recourse to them, in order to supply the deficiencies of the other.

But the most pernicious of all taxes are the arbitrary, They are commonly converted by their management, into punishments on industry; and also, by their unavoidable inequality, are more grievous, than by the real burden which

they impose. It is surprising, therefore, to see them have place among any civilized people. DAVID HUME
Of Taxes, 1752

[177] When wages are fixed by what is called a law, the legal wages remain stationary, while everything else is in progression; and as those who make that law still continue to lay on new taxes by other laws, they increase the expence of living by one law and take away the means by another.

THOMAS PAINE
The Rights of Man, 1792

[178] The State may make a good or a bad use of the taxes which it levies. When it renders to the public services which are the equivalent to the value it receives, it makes a good use of them. And when it dissipates its revenues without giving any service in return, it makes a bad use of them.

FREDERIC BASTIAT
Economic Sophisms, 1845

[179] Income tax evasion is a legal, not a moral question. Anyone has a right to do anything the law does not say is wrong. You only do what you are compelled to do by law. It is no pleasure to pay taxes. It is just as bad to pay too much as too little. J. PIERPONT MORGAN
1866–1945

[180] A tax, in as far as the thing taxed is abstained from, operates as a prohibition: as a discouragement to that branch of trade or production to which the thing belongs, and as an encouragement to rival branches, that is more or less to all other branches. Hence another head of connection between finance and political economy in its narrower sense. The same illusion which has recommended the

encouragement of particular branches of wealth as a means of increase to the whole, has led to the exaggeration of the bad effect of taxes in this point of view. Hence the care taken by governments to throw the weight of taxes upon imports and home productions rather than upon exports: that is, upon their own subjects rather than upon foreigners.

JEREMY BENTHAM
An Institute of Political Economy, 1801–04

[181] Taxes . . . prevent the national capital from being distributed in the way most beneficial to the community. For the general prosperity, there cannot be too much facility given to the conveyance and exchange of all kinds of property, as it is by such means that capital of every specie is likely to find its way into the hands of those who will best employ it in increasing the productions of the country.

DAVID RICARDO
The Principles of Political Economy and Taxation, 1821

[182] The schoolboy whips his taxed top; the beardless youth manages his taxed horse with a taxed bridle on a taxed road; and the dying Englishman, pouring his medicine, which has paid seven per cent, into a spoon that has paid fifteen per cent, flings himself back upon his chintz bed which has paid twenty-five per cent, and expires in the arms of an apothecary who has paid a licence of a hundred pounds for the privilege of putting him to death.

REV. SYDNEY SMITH
Review of Seybert's Annals of the United States, 1820

[183] Economists (and economic advisers) have for long been inclined to assume that anything can be done with the taxation weapon. Balance-of-payments crises and other

inflationary troubles only arise because governments do not have the courage to wield this weapon resolutely enough. By a firm enough use of 'fiscal policy' it is often assumed, any economy can be controlled. Experience however is beginning to belie this optimism. It now appears that there are limits to what can be done with fiscal policy as a 'regulator', limits that show themselves in (at least) two ways.

One concerns the reaction of the taxpayer who is not 'living from hand to mouth', but is either saving currently or has a cushion of past savings on which he can fall back. It is only too likely that when he is exposed to an additional tax (proclaimed as a temporary tax to meet an emergency), he will conclude that this is precisely the sort of occasion for which he has his cushion. Whatever the form in which the tax is imposed, he is not *obliged* to change his consumption pattern. He can pay the tax out of capital or out of additions to his capital which he would otherwise have made. This is perfectly rational behaviour on the assumption (hoped on all hands to be correct) that the crisis will not last for ever, so that he will have an opportunity for righting his capital position on easier terms later on. It is not only the 'wealthy', but quite a large part of the tax-paying population, who are likely to respond to a considerable extent in this manner. So far as they are concerned the weapon of taxation is not effective for the purpose in question. SIR JOHN HICKS

After the Boom, 1966

[184] Whatever habit has rendered delightful, will be relinquished with reluctance, and will continue to be consumed notwithstanding a very heavy tax; but this reluctance has its limits, and experience every day demonstrates that an increase in the nominal amount of taxation, often

diminishes the produce. One man will continue to drink the same quantity of wine, though the price of every bottle should be raised three shillings, who would yet relinquish the use of wine rather than pay four. Another will be content to pay four, yet refuse to pay five shillings. The same may be said of other taxes on luxuries: many would pay a tax of £5 for the enjoyment which a horse affords, who would not pay £10 or £20. It is not because they cannot pay more, but because they will not pay more. Every man has some standard in his own mind by which he estimates the value of his enjoyments, but that standard is as various as the human character. DAVID RICARDO

The Principles of Political Economy and Taxation, 1817

[185] Any tax which shall have the effect of raising wages, will be paid by a diminution of profits, and therefore . . . a tax on wages is in fact a tax on profits. DAVID RICARDO

The Principles of Political Economy and Taxation, 1817

[186] A country which has been forced by the folly of the rapacity of its own government, or by the folly or rapacity of other States, to raise a large public revenue, suffers in general far more from the indirect than from the direct effects of taxation; suffers more by being prevented from producing, than by being obliged to pay.

NASSAU WILLIAM SENIOR

An Outline of the Science of Political Economy, 1836

[187] A protective duty is a tax directed against a foreign product; but we must never forget that it falls back on the home consumer. Now the consumer is the tax-payer. The agreeable language you address to him is this: 'Because your taxes are heavy, we raise the price of everything you

buy; because the State lays hold of one part of your income, we hand over another to the monopolists.'

FREDERIC BASTIAT
Economic Sophisms, 1845

[188] There is strong evidence to suggest that if people realized just how much of their earnings they are giving to the government they would be angry and horrified. Can one imagine the results of a social survey which asked people of all classes, 'How much of your income do you wish to give to government?', returning the answer 'Just under half'. The idea is preposterous, almost as preposterous as that which suggests that one can collect nearly 40 per cent of the national income through a progressive taxation system. Any such attempt must bear extremely heavily on people with lower incomes if only because if it does not do so the wealthier, more knowledgeable, and enterprising elements will quit the country. We should therefore seriously aim at conducting the business of government on a budget of not more than 25 per cent of the national income, at all times except war, or similar emergency. COLIN CLARK
'Taxation for Expansion', in *Rebirth of Britain*, 1964

[189] To tax and to please, no more than to love and to be wise, is not given to men. EDMUND BURKE
Speech on American Taxation, 1774

[190] My favourite quotation from the New China News Agency has always been: 'The peasants are enthusiastically paying their taxes.'
Letter in *The Times*, February 1969

IV

Attitudes to Work

[191] What is work? Work is struggle. MAO TSE-TUNG
Quotations, 1945

[192] I understand by *labour* the application of our faculties to the satisfaction of our wants. FREDERIC BASTIAT
Harmonies of Political Economy, 1860

[193] Hitherto it is questionable if all the mechanical inventions yet made have lightened the day's toil of any human being. They have enabled a greater proportion to live the same life of drudgery and imprisonment and an increased number of manufacturers and others to make fortunes. They have increased the comforts of the middle classes. But they have not yet begun to effect those great changes in human destiny, which it is in their nature and their futurity to accomplish. JOHN STUART MILL
Principles of Political Economy, 1848

[194] John Stuart Mill says in his Principles of Political Economy: 'It is questionable if all the mechanical inventions yet made have lightened the day's toil of any human being.' That is, however, by no means the aim of the capitalistic application of machinery. Like every other increase in the productiveness of labour, machinery is intended to cheapen commodities, and, by shortening that portion of the working day in which the labourer works for himself, to lengthen the other portion that he gives without an equivalent to the capitalist. In short, it is a means for producing surplus-value. KARL MARX
Capital, 1867

[195] Nothing shall be reckoned to a man but that for which he hath made efforts.

The Koran, An-Najm 39

[196] Produce! Produce! Were it but the pitifullest infinitesimal fraction of a product, produce it in God's name! 'Tis the utmost thou hast in thee: out with it, then!

THOMAS CARLYLE
Sartor Resartus, 1833

[197] Even in the meanest sorts of Labour, the whole soul of a man is composed into a kind of real harmony the instant he sets himself to work.

THOMAS CARLYLE
Past and Present, 1843

[198] If your peasant love the fields which give him bread, he will not think it hard to labour in them; his toil will no longer be as that of the beast, but upward looking and touched with light from other than the visible heavens. . . .

GEORGE GISSING
The Private Papers of Henry Ryecroft, 1903

[199] There is a cant abroad at the present day, that there is a special pleasure in industry, and hence we are taught to regard all those who object to work as appertaining to the class of natural vagabonds; but where is the man among us who loves labour? For work or labour is merely that which is irksome to perform and which every man requires a certain remuneration to induce him to perform. If men really loved work they would pay to be allowed to do it rather than require to be paid for doing it.

HENRY MAYHEW
London Labour and the London Poor, 1861–62

[200] Free human beings are not brought up to their work on the same principles as a machine, a horse, or a slave.

ALFRED MARSHALL
Principles of Economics, 1890

[201] There is no point in work
unless it absorbs you
like an absorbing game.
If it doesn't absorb you,
if it's never any fun,
don't do it.

D. H. LAWRENCE
From 'Work', *Pansies*, 1929

[202] Let us but trace some of the ordinary provisions of life . . . and see how much they receive of their value from human industry. Bread, wine and cloth are things of daily use and great plenty, yet notwithstanding, acorns, water, and leaves, or skins must be our bread, drink and clothing, did not labour furnish us with these more useful commodities. For whatever bread is worth more than acorns, wine than water, and cloth and silk than leaves, skins or moss, that is wholly owing to labour and industry.

JOHN LOCKE
Civil Government, 1690

[203] One of the most essential principles of communism consists in the idea, empirically based on human nature, that differences of *brainpower* and of intellectual faculties in general entail no differences at all in food-*capacity* and physical needs; and that, consequently, the false maxim, based on existing conditions—'to each according to his abilities'—must so far as it relates to entitlement in the strict sense of the term, be amended to give another maxim: '*To each according to his needs.*' In other words, difference in activity, in type of work, is no ground for inequality, or for any *privilege* in regard to possession or entitlement.

MARX AND ENGELS
The German Ideology, 1845–46

[204] In practice nobody cares whether work is useful or useless, productive or parasitic; the sole thing demanded is that it shall be profitable. . . . A beggar, looked at realistically, is simply a business man, getting his living, like other business men, in the way that comes to hand. He has not, more than most modern people, sold his honour; he has merely made the mistake of choosing a trade at which it is impossible to grow rich.

GEORGE ORWELL
Down and Out in Paris and London, 1933

[205] Great nations are never impoverished by private, though they sometimes are by public, prodigality and misconduct. The whole, or almost the whole public revenue, is in most countries, employed in maintaining unproductive hands. . . . Such people, as they themselves produce nothing, are all maintained by the product of other men's labour.

ADAM SMITH
The Wealth of Nations, 1776

[206] Under the Roman empire, the labour of an industrious and ingenious people was variously, but incessantly, employed in the service of the rich. In their dress, their table, their houses and their furniture, the favourites of fortune united every refinement of conveniency, of elegance, and of splendour, whatever could soothe their pride or gratify their sensuality. Such refinements, under the odious name of luxury, have been severely arraigned by the moralists of every age; and it might perhaps be more conducive to the virtue, as well as happiness, of mankind, if all possessed the necessaries, and none the superfluities, of life. But in the present imperfect condition of society, luxury, though it may proceed from vice or folly, seems to be the only means

that can correct the unequal distribution of property. The diligent mechanic, and the skilful artist, who have obtained no share in the division of the earth, receive a voluntary tax from the possessors of land; and the latter are prompted, by a sense of interest, to improve those estates, with whose produce they may purchase additional pleasures. This operation, the particular effects of which are felt in every society, acted with much more diffusive energy in the Roman world. The provinces would soon have been exhausted of their wealth, if the manufacturers and commerce of luxury had not insensibly restored to the industrious subjects the sums which were exacted from them by the arms and authority of Rome. As long as the circulation was confined within the bounds of the empire, it impressed the political machine with a new degree of activity, and its consequences, sometimes beneficial, could never become pernicious.

EDWARD GIBBON
The Decline and Fall of the Roman Empire, 1776–87

[207] The friends of humanity cannot but wish that in all countries the labouring classes should have a taste for comforts and enjoyments, and that they should be stimulated by all legal means in their exertions to procure them. There cannot be a better security against a superabundant population. In those countries where the labouring classes have the fewest wants, and are contented with the cheapest food, the people are exposed to the greatest vicissitudes and miseries.

DAVID RICARDO
The Principles of Political Economy and Taxation, 1817

[208] Masters are always and every where in a sort of tacit, but constant and uniform, combination not to raise the

wages of labour above their actual rate. To violate this combination is every where a most unpopular action, and a sort of reproach to a master among his neighbours and equals. We seldom, indeed, hear of this combination, because it is the usual, and one may say, the natural state of things which nobody ever hears of. Masters too sometimes enter into particular combinations to sink the wages of labour even below this rate. These are always conducted with the utmost silence and secrecy, till the moment of execution, and when the workmen yield, as they sometimes do, without resistance, though severely felt by them, they are never heard of by other people. ADAM SMITH

The Wealth of Nations, 1776

[209] If a country can only be rich by running a successful race for low wages, I should be disposed to say at once, perish such riches. THOMAS ROBERT MALTHUS

Principles of Political Economy, 1820

[210] Every action which tends to make the labourer put up with less comfort, or less security, tends to lower his wages. Teach him nothing, so that he wants no books nor other pleasures of the mind. Abolish bodily amusements, so that he expects no pleasures of the body. Accustom him to live like a beast in a hovel; remove all fear of absolute starvation by a poor-law; use the same machinery to persuade him that he may, with a good conscience, desert helpless children or old parents; give him little doles at every pinch, lest he be tempted to rebel;—do all this, and your dull aimless wretch will plod from day to day, expecting nothing more, and spawning swarms of wretched beings to succeed him in his hopeless contentment with a pittance.

. . . Let him look on miscalled charity as a temptation of the devil; and add to all this the greatest want of all, the longing that he may be that excellent thing, the man who walks in the ways of God; and never fear that this being will grovel out a life of hardship, or fail to learn how to win that which he so much desires. FLEEMING JENKIN

Essays on Political Economy, 1887

[211] All historical and theoretical evidence points to the conclusion that a 'free' system in modern conditions needs at least 10 per cent, but more probably 15 to 20 per cent unemployment for stability, that is to say an industrial reserve army of between 1½ and 2½ million.

THOMAS BALOGH

New Statesman, 24 January, 1948

[212] Nature constructs no machines, no locomotives, railways, electric telegraphs, self-acting mules, etc. They are the products of human industry, natural materials, transformed into instruments of the human domination of Nature, or of its activity in Nature. They are instruments of the human brain created by the human hand; they are the materialized power of knowledge. The development of fixed capital indicates the extent to which general social knowledge has become a direct force of production, and thus the extent to which the conditions of the social life process have been brought under the control of the general intellect and reconstructed in accordance with it. It shows to what degree the social forces of production are produced, not only in the form of knowledge, but also as direct instruments of social practice and of the real-life process. KARL MARX

Grundrisse der Kritik der Politischen Oekonomic, 1857

[213] Work is not done for its own sake. Marx always spoke of Communist labour as an activity which would be highly interesting, thought-inspiring, a constant source of fantasy, initiative and desire for new things. It must be an activity the accomplishment and results of which give people the greatest measure of satisfaction. OTA SIK

'Socialist Market Relations', in *Socialism, Capitalism and Economic Growth*, 1967

[214] Man cannot create material things. In the mental and moral world indeed he may produce new ideas; but when he is said to produce material things, he really only produces utilities; or in other words, his efforts and sacrifices result in changing the form or arrangement of matter to adapt it better for the satisfaction of wants. ALFRED MARSHALL

Principles of Economics, 1890

[215] It is in vain to say that all mouths which the increase of mankind calls into existence bring with them hands. The new mouths require as much food as the old ones, and the hands do not produce as much. JOHN STUART MILL

Principles of Political Economy, 1848

[216] 'It's the mistake you lads make that have got nothing either in your brains or your pockets, to think you've got a better start in the world if you stick yourselves in a place where you can keep your coats clean, and have the shop-wenches take you for a fine gentleman. That isn't the way I started, young man: when I was sixteen, my jacket smelt of tar, and I wasn't afraid of handling cheeses. That's the reason I can wear good broadcloth now, and have my legs under the same table with the heads of the best firms. . . .'

GEORGE ELIOT

Mr Deane in *The Mill on the Floss*, 1860

[217] Labour is the contest of the life of man with an opposite; the term 'life' including his intellect, soul, and physical power, contending with question, difficulty, trial, or material force. Labour is of a higher or lower order, as it includes more or fewer of the elements of life; and labour of good quality, in any kind, includes always as much intellect and feeling as will fully and harmoniously regulate the physical force.

JOHN RUSKIN
'Ad Valorem', *Unto This Last*, 1862

[218] One of the most strongly marked features of the English people is their spirit of industry, standing out prominent and distinct in their past history, and as strikingly characteristic of them now as at any former period. It is this spirit, displayed by the commons of England, which has laid the foundation and built up the industrial greatness of the empire. This vigorous growth of the nation has been mainly the result of the free energy of individuals, and it has been contingent upon the hands and minds from time to time actively employed within it, whether as cultivators of the soil, producers of articles of utility, contrivers of tools and machines, writers of books, or creators of works of art. And while this spirit of active industry has been the vital principle of the nation, it has also been the saving and remedial one, counteracting from time to time the effects of errors in our laws and imperfections in our constitution. . . .

By labour the earth has been subdued, and man redeemed from barbarism; nor has a single step in civilization been made without it. Labour is not only a necessity and a duty, but a blessing.

SAMUEL SMILES
Self-Help, 1859

[219] It is true that we have lost the capital influx from

overseas investments, and that 'the Continent will not suffer England to be the workshop of the world'. (This warning, incidentally, was uttered . . . by Disraeli in 1838.) But it is equally true that fifteen years ago West Germany was truncated, lying in ruins and flooded by several million refugees; that France too lost its empire and has only just emerged from its seven years' war with Algeria; that even little Austria, a torso from which all four limbs have been amputated, is running merrily about in its self-propelled invalid chair. What ails Britain is not the loss of Empire but the loss of incentive. We hear the news at nine o'clock, but where are the eagles and the trumpets?

ARTHUR KOESTLER
'The Lion and the Ostrich', *Encounter*, July 1963

[220] The English like a comfortable life compared with our German standards. This does not mean that they are incapable of sustained efforts, but they avoid them so far as they can. . . .

Münchener Zeitung, 16 May, 1936.
(Quoted by Churchill in *The Second World War*, Vol. 1, 1948)

[221] The test of a people is what they can do when they're tired.

WINSTON CHURCHILL
1874–1965

[222] The principle that a man has a right to the produce of his own labour is useless in an industrial civilization. Suppose you are employed in one operation in the manufacture of Ford cars, how is anyone to estimate what proportion of the total output is due to your labour? Or suppose you are employed by a railway company in the transport of goods, who can decide what share you shall

be deemed to have in the production of the goods? Such considerations have led those who wish to prevent the exploitation of labour to abandon the principle of the right to your own produce in favour of more Socialistic methods of organizing production and distribution.

BERTRAND RUSSELL
A History of Western Philosophy, 1946

[223] The idea that all wealth is produced by manual workers, and that all income from property is drawn from the results of labour, is very widely held among the workers, whether they call themselves socialists or not. A manual worker regards himself as a man who gives more than he gets, while others are getting more than they deserve. By producing the whole product, as he thinks he does, he produces the profit gained by it; any profit he does not get, then, is deducted from his proper wages. The average worker now watches carefully the changes in the profits of his company, and if he thinks that they have increased beyond what he regards as fair, he claims an increase in wages. The antithetical character of wages and profits (he does not think about rent and interest) is something which he feels rather than a doctrine inculcated in him.

His ideas of the class struggle are not just a theory for him but something derived from his own experience. Every small concession which he gained was obtained not through charity or argument or out of sympathy, but by the struggle of a strong organization determined to fight for his rights.

FERDYNAND ZWEIG
The British Worker, 1952

[224] Equal quantities of labour, at all times and places, may be said to be of equal value to the labourer. In his

ordinary state of health, strength and spirits; in the ordinary degree of his skill and dexterity, he must always lay down the same portion of his ease, his liberty, and his happiness. The price which he pays must always be the same, whatever may be the quantity of goods which he receives in return for it.

ADAM SMITH
Lectures on Justice, etc. (1763), published 1896

[225] To work at the bidding and for the profit of another, without any interest in the work—the price of their labour being adjusted by hostile competition, one side demanding as much and the other paying as little as possible—is not, even when wages are high, a satisfactory state to human beings of educated intelligence who have ceased to think themselves naturally inferior to those whom they serve.

JOHN STUART MILL
Principles of Political Economy, 1848

[226] 'I should think myself a very bad woman, if I had done what I do for a farthing less.'

JOSEPH ADDISON
The Drummer, 1715

[227] If a man can bring to London an ounce of silver out of the earth of Peru in the same time that he can produce a bushel of corn, then one is the natural price of the other; now if by reason of new and more easier mines a man can get two ounces of silver as easily as he formerly did one, then corn will be as cheap at ten shillings as it was before at five shillings, *ceteris paribus*.

SIR WILLIAM PETTY
Verbum Sapienti, 1692 (posthumous)

[228] It is satisfactory to think that a multitude of people are toiling in the harvest fields in order that we may talk of Polynesia. Like every other good thing in this world,

leisure and culture have to be paid for. Fortunately, however, it is not the leisured and the cultured who have to pay. Let us be duly thankful for that. . . .'

ALDOUS HUXLEY
Crome Yellow, 1921

[229] It is a violent method, and in most cases impracticable, to oblige the labourer in toil, to order to raise from the land more than what subsists himself and the family. Furnish him with manufactures and commodities, and he will do it of himself. Afterwards you will find it easy to seize some part of his superfluous labour, and employ it in the public service, without giving him his wonted return. Being accustomed to industry, he will think this less grievous, than if, at once, you obliged him to an augmentation of labour without any reward. The case is the same with regard to the other members of the state. The greater is the stock of labour of all kinds, the greater quantity may be taken from the heap, without making any sensible alteration in it.

DAVID HUME
Of Commerce, 1752

[230] Skilled labour counts only as simple labour intensified, or, rather, as multiplied simple labour, a given quantity of skilled being considered equal to a greater quantity of simple labour. Experience shows that this reduction is constantly being made. A commodity may be the product of the most skilled labour, but its value, by equating it to the product of simple unskilled labour, represents a definite quantity of the latter labour alone. The different proportions in which different sorts of labour are reduced to unskilled labour as their standard are established by a social process

which goes on behind the backs of the producers, and consequently appears to be fixed by custom. For simplicity's sake we shall henceforth account every kind of labour to be simple unskilled labour; by this we can do no more than save ourselves the trouble of making the reduction.

KARL MARX
Capital, 1867

[231] The welfare state does not eliminate the need for self-help. It is properly concerned with safeguarding individuals from the insecurities of industrialism and liberating them from the inequalities of opportunity, but it can only provide a floor and not a ceiling. Its objective, properly understood, is to liberate men to realize their own full gifts, not to pamper them or make them dependent. ASA BRIGGS
Introduction to 1958 edition of *Self-Help* by Samuel Smiles (1858)

[232] Combination is an awful power. It is like the equally mighty agency of steam; capable of almost unlimited good or evil. But to obtain a blessing on its labours, it must work under the direction of a high and intelligent will; incapable of being misled by passion or excitement. MRS GASKELL
Mary Barton, 1848

[233] Some economists argue that, as paupers are consumers, they should, whenever they are able to work, be made producers also, or otherwise they exhaust the national wealth, to which they do not contribute. This might be a sound axiom were there work sufficient for all. But in an over-populated country there is not work enough, as is proven by the mere fact of the over-population; and the able-bodied paupers *are* paupers simply *because they cannot obtain work*, so that to employ those who are out of work is to

throw out those who are in work, and thus to pauperize the self-supporting. HENRY MAYHEW
London Labour and the London Poor, 1861–62

[234] I pay my servants exactly what wages I think necessary to make them comfortable. The sum is not determined at all by competition; but sometimes by my notions of their comfort and deserving, and sometimes by theirs. If I were to become penniless tomorrow, several of them would certainly still serve me for nothing. JOHN RUSKIN
Preface to *Munera Pulveris*, 1880

[235] It may be regrettable, but it seems to be a fact that people's enthusiasm about almost any group to which they belong is enhanced by competition. HUGH GAITSKELL
Socialism and Nationalisation, 1956

[236] Society, which is the beginning and basis of morals, exists simply for the concentration of human energy, and in order to ensure its own continuance and healthy stability it demands, and no doubt rightly demands, of each of its citizens that he should contribute some form of productive labour to the common weal, and toil and travail that the day's work may be done. Society often forgives the criminal; it never forgives the dreamer. The beautiful sterile emotions that art excites in us, are hateful in its eyes, and so completely are people dominated by the tyranny of this dreadful social ideal that they are always coming shamelessly up to one at Private Views and other places that are open to the general public, and saying in a loud stentorian voice, 'What are you doing?' whereas 'What are you thinking?' is the only question that any single civilized being should ever be allowed to whisper to another. OSCAR WILDE
'The True Function of Criticism', *The Nineteenth Century*, September 1890

[237] Forty years ago people were all talking about emigration. Why do not the people emigrate? people asked. There were societies for promoting emigration. I read only two or three days ago an article in the *Fortnightly Review*, a review of the life of the late Canon Kingsley, and I found he said that thirty or forty years ago all thoughtful people were appalled at the state of the country. They thought something was going to happen, the state of the country was so bad. The people suffered so much, they were so discontented, that there would before long be a great catastophe, like a general insurrection or revolution; and people said, why cannot millions go to a country where there is room for them?

The people have emigrated, of course, as an active-minded people like this always will emigrate. But emigration has not made this great change. People are far more numerous in the country now than they were then, and yet for all that, they are much better off, there is much greater demand for labour, and the rate of wages in every branch of labour is higher than it was at that time. JOHN BRIGHT

Speech at Rochdale on 2 January, 1877

[238] Every permanent improvement of the soil, every railway and road, every bettering of the general condition of society, every facility given for production, every stimulus supplied to consumption, raises rent. The landowner sleeps but thrives. He alone among the recipients in the distribution of products, owes everything to the labour of others, contributes nothing of his own. He inherits part of the fruits of present industry, and has appropriated the lion's share of accumulated intelligence. THOROLD ROGERS

Manual of Political Economy (2nd edn.), 1869

[239] Every consumer at home and abroad in the price of the product he buys will, through the added cost of shorter hours, pay equally with the manufacturer and the producer for the maintenance of people that without these shorter hours would be unemployed, and the cost of which would be borne by the producers alone. Absorption of the unemployed by general reduction of hours, this followed by municipalization of industry and nationalization of monopolies, is the line of least resistance for all. It is regulation or riot, reduction or revolution. JOHN BURNS

'The Labour Question', *The Nineteenth Century*, December 1892

[240] 'I hold it', said Mr Saunders, 'to be one of the great triumphs of our day, that it has so subordinated all the vague and more lawless sentiments to the solid guidance of sober economical consideration. And not only do I consider a cotton-mill, but I consider a good sewer, to be a far nobler and a far holier thing—for holy in reality does but mean healthy—that the most admired Madonna ever painted.'

'A good sewer', said Mr Herbert, 'is, I admit, an entirely holy thing. . . .' W. H. MALLOCK

The New Republic, 1877

[241] How, then, does the English bourgeoise and the government and press which are associated with it regard pauperism? In so far as the English bourgeoisie blames politics for the existence of pauperism, the Whig accuses the Tory, while the Tory accuses the Whig, of being responsible for it. According to the Whig, the chief cause of pauperism is the monopoly exercised by the great landowners and the laws prohibiting the import of corn. According to the Tory, the whole evil springs from liberalism, from competition, and from the too greatly extended

factory system. Neither of the parties regards politics in general as a cause, but each one only the policy of the other party; neither party even dreams of a reform of society.

The most convincing expression of English opinion on pauperism—we are still referring to the opinion of the English bourgeoisie and government—is English political economy, that is to say, the scientific reflection of English economic circumstances. KARL MARX

Article in *Vorwarts*, 7 August, 1844

[242] We are the most *lazy diligent* nation in the world. Vast trade, rich manufactures, mighty wealth, universal correspondence and happy success have been constant companions of England, and given us the title of an industrious people, and so in general we are.

But there is a general taint of slothfulness upon our poor; there's nothing more frequent, than for the Englishman to work till he has got his pocket full of money, and then go and be idle, *or perhaps drunk*, till 'tis all gone, and perhaps himself in debt. . . .

'Tis the men that *won't work*, not the men that *can get no work*, which makes the numbers of our Poor; all the workhouses in England, and all the overseers setting up stocks and manufactures, won't reach this case. DANIEL DEFOE

Giving Alms No Charity, 1704

[243] Surely there should be a power, if there be a means, of at least compelling every man to bear his own share in the burden of natural providence, instead of allowing him to cast it on the shoulders of others? When instances can be given, as I can give from my own personal knowledge, of young labourers by the dozen without a change of decent

clothes, continually and brutally drinking, and living almost like savages, while earning fully a pound a week—or, as I can also give, of a carter-boy, *aged fourteen years*, spending three shillings a week regularly on tobacco—it is quite time that poor, decent provident people should demur to being taxed for the infallible necessities of such a generation, and that the public ear should at least be open wide to hear any suggestions which may tend to the redress of so gross an injustice, and the blotting out of such a national disgrace.

For it is a plain failure of good government that an enormous class of people should be allowed to ignore the first duty of every loyal citizen, and it is a political crime of the gravest sort that they should be, as they are, encouraged in the notion that the grosser their waste, their sensuality, their ignorance, and their selfishness, the stronger claim they establish to support and aid from their fellow-men. I am certain to carry every ratepayer in England with me when I say that our present system is, in its working, most unreasonable and unjust, and that something should be done to make the wasteful bear at least a part of the burden so unfairly laid upon the shoulders of the thrifty.

I do not see for an instant why we should mince this matter. If the labouring classes can make their own provision, and will do so, let them be shown how; if they can, and will not, let them be compelled.

WILLIAM LEWERY BLACKLEY
'National Insurance: A Cheap, Practical, and Popular Means of Abolishing Poor Rates', *The Nineteenth Century*, 1878

[244] Failure to work, even when it could be afforded, was offensive to what came to be called the Victorian, but could as well have been named the economic, morality. 'To

live in idleness, even if you have the means, is not only injurious to yourself, but a species of fraud upon the community.'

But if the goods have ceased to be urgent, where is the fraud? Can the North Dakota farmer be indicted for failure to labour hard and long to produce the wheat that his government wishes passionately it did not have to buy? Are we desperately dependent on the diligence of the worker who applies maroon and pink enamel to the functionless bulge of a modern motorcar? The idle man may still be an enemy of himself, But it is hard to say that the loss of his effort is damaging to society. Yet it is such damage which causes us to condemn idleness.

JOHN KENNETH GALBRAITH
The Affluent Society, 1958

[245] It is not, I think, irrational or overdrawn to suggest that there is an analogy between the price or wage that used to be paid in the nineteenth century for the labourers' hire and the prices now paid for primary products. Both rewards are determined by the relative strength of the bargainers and just as, in the nineteenth century, the owners and managers held most of the cards, so, today, the bargaining strength lies in the main with the North Atlantic consumer who controls the investment, earns the dividends and provides the bulk of the market for the primary producers. In both cases, the workers without the bargaining cards gain least from the exchange.

BARBARA WARD
Poverty and Politics, 1969

V

Benefits of Trade

[246] The onlie meanes to cause muche bullione to be brought oute of other realmes unto the kinge's mintes is to provide that a great quantitie of our wares maye be carriede yerely into landes beyonde the Sees and lesse quantitie of their wares be brought hither agene. ANON

Policies to Reduce this Realme of Englande unto a prosperus Wealthe and Estate, 1549

[247] The matter of trade is either natural or artificial. The natural matter of commerce is merchandise, which merchants from the end of trade have stiled commodities. The artificial matter of commerce is money, which has obtained the title of sinews of war and of state.

EDWARD MISSENDEN
Free Trade, 1622

[248] It is not our conquests, but our commerce, it is not our swords, but our sails that first spread the English name in Barbary, Turkey, Armenia, Muscovy, Arabia, Persia, India, China, and indeed over and about the world; it is the traffic of our merchants and the boundless desire of that nation to eternize the English honour and name that has induced them to sail and seek into all corners of the earth.

LEWES ROBERTS
Treasure of Trafficke, 1641

[249] Although a kingdom may be enriched by gifts received or by purchase taken from some other Nations, yet these are things uncertain and of small consideration when they happen. The ordinary means therefore to increase our Wealth and Treasure is by Forraign Trade, wherein wee must ever observe this rule: to sell more to strangers yearly than wee consume of theirs in value. For suppose that when

this Kingdom is plentifully served with the Cloth, Lead, Tinn, Iron, Fish and other native commodities, wee doe yearly export the overplus to forraign Countries to the value of twenty-two hundred thousand pounds; by which means we are enabled beyond the Seas to buy and bring in forraign wares for our use and Consumptions, to the value of twenty hundred thousand pounds; By this order kept in our trading, we may rest assured that the Kingdom shall be enriched yearly two hundred thousand pounds, which must be brought to us in so much Treasure; because that part of our stock which is not returned to us in wares must necessarily be brought home in treasure. THOMAS MUN

England's Treasure by Forraign Trade, or the Ballance of our Forraign Trade is the Rule of our Treasure, 1664

[250] Laws restraining trade, foreign or domestic, relating to money or other merchandise, are not the ingredients to make a people rich, abounding in money and stock. . . . No people ever yet grew rich by policies, but it is peace, industry, and freedom that bring trade and wealth.

SIR DUDLEY NORTH

A Discourse upon Trade, 1690

[251] If we consult history, we shall find, that, in most nations, foreign trade has preceded any refinement in home manufactures, and given birth to domestic luxury. The temptation is stronger to make use of foreign commodities, which are ready for use, and which are entirely new to us, than to make improvements on any domestic commodity, which always advance by slow degrees, and never affect us by their novelty. The profit is also very great, in exporting what is superfluous at home, and what bears no price, to foreign nations, whose soil or climate is not favourable to that

commodity. Thus men become acquainted with the *pleasures* of luxury and the *profits* of commerce; and are *delicacy* and *industry*, being once awakened, carry them on to farther improvements, in every branch of domestic as well as foreign trade.

DAVID HUME
Of Commerce, 1752

[252] Bachelors and spinsters I decidedly venerate. The world is overstocked with featherless birds. More men than corn is a fearful pre-eminence, the sole and fruitful cause of penury, disease and war, plague, pestilence and famine.

THOMAS LOVE PEACOCK
Melincourt, 1817

[253] Suppose, that all the money of Great Britain were multiplied fivefold in a night. . . . Must not all labour and commodities rise to such an exorbitant height, that no neighbouring nations could afford to buy from us; while their commodities, on the other hand, became comparatively so cheap, that, in spite of all the laws which could be formed, they would be run in upon us, and our money flow out; till we fall to a level with foreigners, and lose that great superiority of riches, which had laid us under such disadvantages?

DAVID HUME
Of the Balance of Trade, 1752

[254] Were our narrow and malignant politics to meet with success, we should reduce all our neighbouring nations to the same state of sloth and ignorance that prevails in Morocco and the coast of Barbary. But what would be the consequence? They could send us no commodities: They could take none from us: Our domestic commerce itself would languish for want of emulation, example and instruction:

And we ourselves should soon fall into the same subject condition to which we had reduced them. I shall therefore venture to acknowledge, that, not only as a man, but as a British subject, I pray for the flourishing commerce of Germany, Spain, Italy, and even France itself. I am at least certain that Great Britain, and all those nations, would flourish more, did their sovereigns and their ministers adopt such enlarged and benevolent sentiments towards each other.

DAVID HUME
Of the Jealousy of Trade, 1758

[255] You would not know your country again. You left it a private little island living on its means. You would find it the capital of the world.

HORACE WALPOLE
Letter to Sir Horace Mann in Florence, 1763

[256] No theory, economic or political, can now be both insular and secure; foreign thoughts come soon and trouble us. . . .

WALTER BAGEHOT
Economic Studies, 1879

[257] People of the same trade seldom meet together, even for merriment and diversion, but the conversation ends in a conspiracy against the public, or in some contrivance to raise prices.

ADAM SMITH
The Wealth of Nations, 1776

[256] It is folly to buy manufactured good[s]; wise to buy raw materials. Why? because you sell them to yourselves, or, what is still better, to foreigners, manufactured; and the manufacturer's profit is all clear gain to you. What they forget is, that the manufacturer, to carry on his business, must have a capital; and that just so much capital as is

employed in that way, is prevented from being employed in any other.

Hence the perfect inutility and mischievousness of all laws and public measures whatsoever, for the pretended encouragement of trade; all prohibitions of rival foreign trade: bounties in every shape whatsoever, all non-importation agreements and engagements to consume home manufacture in preference to foreign in any other view than to afford temporary relief to temporary distress.

JEREMY BENTHAM
Colonies and Navy, c. 1790

[259] Johnson: 'There is nothing which requires more to be illustrated by Philosophy than Trade does. As to mere wealth, that is to say, money, it is clear that one nation or one individual cannot increase its store but by making another poorer: but trade procures what is more valuable, the reciprocation of the peculiar advantages of different countries.'

JAMES BOSWELL
Life of Johnson, 1791

[260] Dr Wetherell, Master of University College, Oxford, accompanied us home from church; and after he was gone, there came two other gentlemen, one of whom uttered the commonplace complaints, that by the increase of taxes, labour would be dear, other nations would undersell us, and our commerce would be ruined. Johnson (smiling): 'Never fear, Sir. Our commerce is in a very good state; and suppose we had no commerce at all, we could live very well on the produce of our own country.'

JAMES BOSWELL
Life of Johnson, 1791

[261] The most unprofitable of all commerce is that connected with foreign dominion. To a few individuals it may be

beneficial, merely because it is commerce; but to the Nation it is a loss. . . . It does not encrease the general quantity in the world, but operates to lessen it, and as a greater mass would be afloat by relinquishing dominion, the participation without the expence would be more valuable than a greater quantity of it.

But it is impossible to engross commerce by dominion; and therefore it is still more fallacious. It cannot exist in confined channels, and necessarily breaks out by regular or irregular means, that defeat the attempt; and to succeed would be still worse.

THOMAS PAINE
The Rights of Man, 1792

[262] In all my publications, where the matter would admit, I have been an advocate for commerce, because I am a friend of its effects. It is a pacific system, operating to cordialize mankind, by rendering Nations, as well as individuals, useful to each other. As to the mere theoretical reformation, I have never preached it up. The most effectual process is that of improving the condition of man by means of his interest; and it is on this ground that I take my stand.

If commerce were permitted to act to the universal extent it is capable, it would extirpate the system of war, and produce a Revolution in the uncivilized state of Governments. The invention of commerce has arisen since those Governments began, and it is the greatest approach towards universal civilization that has yet been made by any means not immediately flowing from moral principles. . . .

Every kind of destruction or embarrassment serves to lessen the quantity [of commerce], and it matters but little in what part of the commercial world the reduction begins. Like blood, it cannot be taken from any of the parts without being taken from the whole mass in circulation, and all partake of the loss. When the ability in any Nation to buy is destroyed, it equally involves the seller. Could the Government of England destroy the commerce of all other Nations, she would most effectually ruin her own.

It is possible that a Nation may be the carrier for the world, but she cannot be the merchant. She cannot be the seller and buyer of her own merchandise. The ability to buy must reside out of herself; and, therefore, the prosperity of any commercial Nation is regulated by the prosperity of the rest. If they are poor she cannot be rich, and her condition, be it what it may, is an index of the height of the commercial tide of other Nations. THOMAS PAINE

The Rights of Man, 1792

[263] It is obvious . . . that a country, notwithstanding a high comparative price of labour and of materials, may easily stand a competition with foreigners in those commodities to which it can apply a superior capital and machinery with great effect; although such a price of labour and materials might give an undisputed advantage to foreigners in agriculture and some other sorts of produce, where the same saving of labour cannot take place. Consequently such a country may find it cheaper to purchase a considerable part of its supplies of grain from abroad with its manufactures and peculiar products, than to grow the whole at home.

If, from all or any of these causes, a nation becomes habitually dependent on foreign countries for the support of a considerable portion of its population, it must evidently be subjected, while such dependence lasts, to some of those evils which belong to a nation purely manufacturing and commercial. THOMAS ROBERT MALTHUS

An Essay on the Principle of Population, 1795

[264] It may be laid down as a universal maxim, that the system of commercial restriction is always either useless or mischievous; or rather mischievous in every case, in a less degree, or in a greater degree. In the judgement of the purchaser, or the consumer, the goods discouraged must be either better than those which are protected, or not: if not better . . . they will not be bought even though no prohibition exist: here then is uselessness, or mischief in the lesser degree. But the case, and the only probable case, in which the fictitious encouragement will be applied, is that where the goods excluded are better, or in other words cheaper, than those sought to be protected: here is unqualified mischief, mischief in the greater degree.

JEREMY BENTHAM
Observations on the Restrictive and Prohibitory Commercial System, 1821

[265] On the termination of the War, Napoleon's empire was broken up into independent kingdoms, and each state set to work to reimpose on itself the fetters which his powerful hand had broken. Douaniers and preventive-service men were found instruments as efficient in wasting the resources of their own country, and in arresting the improvement of their neighbours, as armies and fleets. The produce of France became contraband in Belgium and Italy, and the produce of Belgium and Italy in France. America solemnized the Peace by a tariff, and England by a corn law. To prohibit whatever is wanted became again the rule in commercial policy.

NASSAU WILLIAM SENIOR
An Outline of the Science of Political Economy, 1836

[266] The economical advantages of commerce are surpassed in importance by those of its effects, which are intellectual

and moral. . . . Commerce first taught nations to see with goodwill the wealth and prosperity of one another. Before, the patriot, unless sufficiently advanced in culture to feel the world his country, wished all countries weak, poor, and ill-governed, but his own; he now sees in their wealth and progress a direct source of wealth and progress in his own country. It is commerce which is rapidly rendering war obsolete, by strengthening and multiplying interests which are in natural opposition to it. And it may be said without exaggeration, that the great extent and rapid increase of international trade, in being the principal guarantee of the peace of the world, is the great permanent security for the uninterrupted progress of the ideas, the institutions, and the character of the human race.

JOHN STUART MILL
Principles of Political Economy, 1848

[267] Restrictions on trade, or on production for purposes of trade, are indeed restraints; and all restraint, *qua* restraint, is an evil; but the restraints in question affect only that part of conduct which society is competent to restrain, and are wrong solely because they do not really produce the results which it is desired to produce by them.

JOHN STUART MILL
On Liberty, 1859

[268] Merchant and pirate were for a long period one and the same person. Even today mercantile morality is really nothing but a refinement of piratical morality.

F. W. NIETZSCHE
Maxims, c. 1878

[269] Do not, however, disparage foreign trade. There is

nothing wrong with foreign trade as such. . . . The necessities of travelling and trade, and the common interest of all nations in the works and discoveries of art, have forced them to make international agreements and treaties with one another which are making an end of 'keeping ourselves to ourselves', and throwing half-bricks at foreigners and strangers. Honest foreign trade would never have got us into trouble. BERNARD SHAW

The Intelligent Woman's Guide to Socialism and Capitalism, 1928

[270] The British Empire has been mainly founded by traders organized in companies. The advantages of company trading lay in the fact that a company does not die, and so there is a continuity of existence. When trading with undeveloped peoples, a corporation with a long life becomes a name and a power. Companies could also provide relays of capital if necessary as individuals could not. They could and did take risks that no Government would face, and they could, being only corporations, withdraw if necessary without loss of prestige in a way that would be impossible to a Government whose national honour would be at once involved. They were, moreover, economical in working as they had not the same standard of expenditure as a Government. Government servants must not make mistakes —it is the unforgivable crime—and so the tendency is naturally to play for safety. Companies, on the other hand, showed a flexibility and initiative and their officers developed a capacity for making sudden decisions that would not have been possible to any civil servant. Companies were, therefore, admirably adapted to do pioneer work, as Governments were later better qualified to organize an administration and to think in terms of future generations untroubled

by questions of dividends or profit and loss of the moment.

L. C. A. KNOWLES
Economic Development of the Overseas Empire, 1928

[271] In a socialist society nobody could possibly doubt that what a nation gets out of international trade is the imports and that the exports are the sacrifice which must be undergone in order to procure the imports, whereas in commercial society this common-sense view is as a rule completely hidden from the man in the street who therefore cheerfully supports policies that are to his disadvantage.

J. A. SCHUMPETER
Capitalism, Socialism and Democracy, 1943

[272] It is not true that in the absence of public intervention there will be no competition. The simplest proof is that all over the world public and private authorities continue to devote much effort to the repression of competition. Governments employ tens of thousands of custom officials to block foreign competition; or seek to confer absolute monopolies upon nationalized industries. Private cartels continue to hunt out competitors in the hope of blocking their activities. Would all this effort to keep it down be necessary if competition did not have a continuing vitality of its own?

JOHN JEWKES
'No Industry Without Enterprise', in *Growth Through Industry*, 1967

[273] Who can tell without instruction what is likely to be the effect of the new loans of England to foreign nations? We press upon half-finished and half-civilized communities incalculable sums. . . . We enable these communities to read in every newspaper that they can have ready money, almost of any amount, on 'personal security'. No incipient and

arrested civilizations ever had this facility before. What will be the effect on such civilizations now, no untutored mind can say. WALTER BAGEHOT
Economic Studies, 1879

[274] The advocacy and operation of foreign aid suggests clearly and often explicitly that material advance depends largely on external grants rather than on the emergence of appropriate human qualities, attitudes, values and also on the removal of institutional constraints. Yet the converse is clear from the experience of individuals and groups throughout the world as well as from the history both of the now developed countries and of poor countries which have progressed in recent decades. The progress of individuals, groups and countries has almost always occurred without external doles. . . . The suggestion that material progress depends on external grants encourages the belief that the prime determinants of development can be had for nothing. This belief is unfounded. Moreover, its espousal retards material progress, especially because it encourages the pauperization of the recipients. P. T. BAUER
Foreign Aid: An Instrument for Progress?, 1965

[275] The main positive effect of international trade on the underdeveloped countries has in fact been to promote the production of primary products; and such production, employing mostly unskilled labour, has come to constitute the bulk of their exports. In these lines, however, they often meet inelastic demands in the export market, often also a demand trend which is not rising very rapidly, and excessive price fluctuations. When, furthermore, population is rapidly rising while the larger part of it lives at or near the

subsistence level—which means that there is no scarcity of unskilled labour—any technological improvement in their export production tends to transfer the advantages from the cheapening of production to the importing countries. Since the demand is often inelastic the market will not be greatly enlarged.

The advice—and assistance—which the poorer countries receive from the richer is, even nowadays, often directed towards increasing their production of primary goods for export. The advice is certainly given in good faith, and it may even be rational from the short-term point of view of one under-developed country seen in isolation. In a broader perspective and from a long-term point of view, what would be rational is above all to increase productivity, incomes and living standards in the larger agricultural subsistence sectors, so as to raise the supply price of labour, and in manufacturing industry. This would engender economic development and raise incomes. GUNNAR MYRDAL

Economic Theory and Under-Developed Regions, 1957

[276] Protection *versus* free trade is going to supersede all political issues for many years to come. From the public point of view we do not regret the advent of the new ferment. This issue will at least force people to think, it will force them to consider new facts, and to apply new assumptions. The absurd notion that the 'natural' channels of trade are necessarily the best will quickly be given up; the notion that 'cheapness' is the only aim in a nation's commerce will also be demolished; the need for investigation and the desirability of deliberate collective regulation will be enormously advertised. All this is to the good and makes

towards economic science, and, we think, collectivism of the best sort. BEATRICE WEBB

Journal for 1903, *Our Partnership*, 1948

[277] You have, I thinke, a phrase of Driving a Trade; and you have, I know, a practise of Driving Away Trade, by other use of money; and you have lost a man, that drove a great Trade, the right way in making the best use of our home-commodity. To fetch in Wine, and Spice, and Silks, is but a drawing of Trade; the right driving of trade is, to vent our owne outwarde; and yet, for the drawing in of that which might justly seeme most behoofefull, that is, of Arts, and Manufactures, to be implyed upon our owne Commodity within the Kingdome, he did his part, diligently at least, if not vehemently, if not passionately. This City is a great Theater, and he acted great and various parts in it; and all well. . . . JOHN DONNE

Sermon on a London Merchant, St Paul's, 1626

VI

Consumption and the Market

[278] The market is a place set apart where men may deceive one another.

ANACHARSIS OF SCYTHIA
c. 600 B.C.

[279] He who monopolizes the market either as a seller or as a buyer shall be punished with eighty blows of the long stick. If any has made profit through such monopolistic schemes, that profit shall be regarded as booty, and he shall be punished as a robber according to the amount of booty.

Law Code of the Ts'ing Dynasty. Quoted in *The Economic Principles of Confucius* by Chen Huan-Chang (1911)

[280] Consumption is the sole end and purpose of all production; and the interest of the producer ought to be attended to, only so far as it may be necessary for promoting that of the consumer. The maxim is so perfectly self-evident that it would be absurd to attempt to prove it.

ADAM SMITH
The Wealth of Nations, 1776

[281] Consumption is the end and final clause of all the economic phenomena, and it is in consumption consequently that we must expect to find their ultimate and definitive solution.

FREDERIC BASTIAT
Economic Sophisms, 1845

[282] There exists no more democratic institution than a market.

J. A. SCHUMPETER
Capitalism, Socialism and Democracy (revised edn.), 1947

[283] The interest of the dealers in any particular branch of trade or manufactures is always in some respects different from, and even opposite to, that of the public. To widen

the market and to narrow the competition is always to the interest of the dealers. To widen the market may frequently be agreeable enough to the interest of the public, but to narrow the competition must always be against it, and can serve only to enable the dealers, by raising their profits above what they naturally would be, to levy, for their own benefit, an absurd tax upon the rest of their fellow-citizens. The proposal of any new law or regulation of commerce which comes from this order ought always to be listened to with great precaution, and ought never be adopted till after having been long and carefully examined, not only with the most scrupulous, but with the most suspicious, attention. It comes from an order of men whose interest is never exactly the same with that of the public, who have generally an interest to deceive and even to oppress the public, and who accordingly have, upon many occasions, both deceived and oppressed it.

ADAM SMITH
The Wealth of Nations, 1776

[284] I don't say that I go as far as all that—I am apt to be more mealy-mouthed! Obviously there is some function in the modern world for trade associations as there is for trade unions. There are humble tasks which they may quite usefully discharge. Nevertheless when I think of the lobbying of pressure groups, when I think of the apparatus of organization of public relations, when I think of the *soi-disant* expert articles which are planted out—my motto is 'Watch out'. Individually, your business man is one of the most admirable animals on this planet. Collectively, he is a protectionist at heart.

LORD ROBBINS
Having quoted the foregoing at an I.E.A. dinner, January 1966

[285] To found a great empire for the sole purpose of raising

up a people of customers, may at first sight appear a project fit only for a nation of shopkeepers. It is, however, a project altogether unfit for a nation of shopkeepers; but extremely fit for a nation whose government is influenced by shopkeepers.

ADAM SMITH
The Wealth of Nations, 1776

[286] Slaves have no motive to labour except the dread of punishment, and can never invent any machine for facilitating their business. Free men, who have a stock of their own, can get anything accomplished which they think may be expedient for carrying on labour. If a carpenter thinks that a plane will serve his purpose better than a knife he may go to a smith and get it made; but if a slave make any such proposal, he is called a lazy rascal, and no experiments are made to give him ease . . . in the ancient world, as the arts were all carried on by slaves, no machinery could be invented, because they had no stock; after the fall of the Roman Empire, too, this was the case all over Europe.

ADAM SMITH
Lectures (ed. 1896)

[287] Of the four sets of operations, Production, Distribution, Exchange and Consumption, which constitute the subject of Political Economy, the first three are means. No man produces for the sake of producing, and nothing further. Distribution, in the same manner, is not performed for the sake of distribution. Things are distributed as also exchanged, to some end. That end is consumption.

JAMES MILL
Elements of Political Economy, 1821

[288] If we now proceed to consider the immediate interest of the consumer, we shall find that it is in perfect harmony with the general interest, with all that the welfare of society

calls for. When the purchaser goes to market he desires to find it well stocked. Let the seasons be propitious for all harvests; let inventions, more and more marvellous, bring within reach a greater and greater number of products and enjoyments; let time and labour be saved; let distances be effaced by the perfection and rapidity of transit; let the spirit of justice and of peace allow of a diminished weight of taxation; let barriers of every kind be removed—in all this the interest of the consumer runs parallel with the public interest.

FREDERIC BASTIAT
Economic Sophisms, 1845

[289] The most wonderful working computer the world has ever known . . . into which are fed millions of facts, not only from all over this country but from all round the globe. The answers tumble out; it tells us what it is most advantageous to import or export; what can be produced economically and competitively and in what quantity and where. This wonderful silent mechanism is the market.

J. ENOCH POWELL,
Speech at Dulwich, February 1964

[290] The market place responds to the tastes of consumers with the goods and services that are saleable, whether the tastes are elevated or depraved. It is unfair to criticize the market place for fulfilling these desires, when clearly the defects lie in the popular tastes themselves. I consider it a cowardly concession to a false extension of the idea of democracy to make *sub rosa* attacks on public tastes by denouncing the people who serve them. It is like blaming the waiters in restaurants for obesity.

GEORGE J. STIGLER
The Intellectual and the Market Place, 1963

[291] You seem to think that the wants and tastes of mankind are always ready for the supply; while I am most decidedly of opinion that few things are more difficult, than to inspire new tastes and wants, particularly out of old materials; that one of the great elements of demand is the value that people set upon commodities, and that the more completely the supply is suited to the demand the higher will this value be, and the more days' labour will it exchange for, or give the power of commanding. . . . I am quite of opinion that *practically* the actual check to produce and population arises more from want of stimulus than want of power to produce.

THOMAS ROBERT MALTHUS
Letter to Ricardo, 1812

[292] No one man is capable, without the aid of society, of supplying his own wants; and those wants, acting upon every individual, impel the whole of them into society, as naturally as gravitation acts to a centre.

But she has gone further, She has not only forced man into society by a diversity of wants which the reciprocal aid of each other can supply, but she has also implanted in him a system of social affections, which, though not necessary to his existence, are essential to his happiness. There is no period in life when this love for society ceases to act. It begins and ends with our being.

If we examine with attention the composition and constitution of man, the diversity of his wants and talents in different men for reciprocally accommodating the wants of each other, his propensity to society, and consequently to preserve the advantages resulting from it, we shall easily discover that a great part of what we call Government is mere imposition.

THOMAS PAINE
The Rights of Man, 1792

E

[293] When it pleased God to create a being made up of wants, and of faculties to supply these wants, it was at the same time decreed that this should be subject to suffering; for, apart from suffering, we could form no idea of wants, and, apart from wants, we could form no idea of utility, or of the use and object of any of our faculties. All that constitutes our greatness has its roots in what constitutes our weakness.

FREDERIC BASTIAT
Harmonies of Political Economy, 1860

[294] The need of a constantly expanding market for its products chases the bourgeoisie over the whole surface of the globe. It must nestle everywhere, settle everywhere, establish connections everywhere.

. . . The bourgeoisie, by the rapid improvement of all instruments of production, by the immensely facilitated means of communication, draws all nations, even the most barbarian, into civilization. The cheap prices of its commodities are the heavy artillery with which it batters down all Chinese walls, with which it forces the barbarians' intensely obstinate hatred of foreigners to capitulate. It compels all nations, on pain of extinction, to adopt the bourgeois mode of production; it compels them to introduce what it calls civilization into their midst, i.e. to become bourgeois themselves. In a word, it creates a world after its own image.

MARX AND ENGELS
The Communist Party Manifesto, 1848

[295] The desirable thing, with a view to the happiness of the common people, seems to be, that their habitual food should be dear, and their wages regulated by it; but that, in a

scarcity or other occasional distress, the cheaper food should be readily and cheerfully adopted.

THOMAS ROBERT MALTHUS
An Essay on the Principle of Population, 1798

[296] Wants exist. This is a fact. It would be puerile to inquire whether we should have been better without wants, and why God has made us subject to them.

FREDERIC BASTIAT
Harmonies of Political Economy, 1860

[297] The final object of political economy, therefore, is to get good method of consumption and great quantity of consumption: in other words, to use everything and to use it nobly.

JOHN RUSKIN
'Ad Valorem', *Unto This Last*, 1862

[298] Human wants and desires are countless in number and very various in kind: but they are generally limited and capable of being satisfied. The uncivilized man indeed has not many more than the brute animal; but every step in his progress upwards increases the variety of his methods of satisfying them. He desires not merely larger quantities of those things; he desires a greater choice of things, and things that will satisfy new wants growing up in him.

The desire for excellence for its own sake graduates down from that of a Newton, or a Stradivarius, to that of the fisherman who, even when no one is looking and he is not in a hurry, delights in handling his craft well, and in the fact that she is well built and responds promptly to his guidance. Desires of this kind exert a great influence on the supply of the highest faculties and the greatest inventions; and they are not unimportant on the side of demand. For a large part of the demand for the most highly skilled professional services and the best work of the mechanical artisan, arises from the delight that people have in the training of their own faculties, and in exercising them by aid of the most delicately adjusted and responsive implements.

ALFRED MARSHALL
Principles of Economics, 1890

[299] It is not clear that the freedom of individual business men to produce what, according to their judgement, consumers will want and will pay for . . . is a bad freedom, and ought to be controlled by governments. I am not prepared to say, therefore, that the capitalistic system as a whole is anarchic.

SIR WILLIAM BEVERIDGE
In *The World's Economic Crisis*, 1932

[300] It appears that the whole of the economic activity of humanity (that vast complex of activities which we call the economic System) consists of nothing else but an immense co-operation of workers or producers to make things and do things which consumers want. When it is described in this way, the economic system may sound quite an admirable thing—perhaps too admirable to agree with our experience of it. But in fact there is nothing necessarily admirable about a co-operation to satisfy the wants of consumers. The wants are usually harmless, but they may be deplorable. the methods of co-operating to satisfy even the most respectable wants are sometimes inefficient and stupid. Yet whether the wants are good or bad, whether production is organized efficiently or not, the description still holds. Economic life is an organization of producers to satisfy the wants of consumers.

J. R. HICKS
The Social Framework (3rd edn.), 1960

[301] I happen to believe that when a society's economic life ceases to be shaped by the interaction of the free decisions of individuals, freedom is in a fair way to disappear from other sides of its existence as well. The terms 'free economy' and 'free society' are to be interchangeable.

J. ENOCH POWELL
Saving in a Free Society, 1960

[302] Political economy does not advance . . . But why? It has always been my own conviction that the reason lies not in any material defect of facts (except as to the single question of money), but in the laxity of some amongst the distinctions which are elementary to the science. For example, that one desperate enormity of vicious logic which takes place in the ordinary application to price of the relation between supply and demand has secured more arguments dispersed through speeches, books, journals, than a long life could fully expose.

THOMAS DE QUINCEY
The Logic of Political Economy, 1844

[303] There has been a long controversy as to whether 'cost of production' or 'utility' governs value. It might as reasonably be disputed whether it is the upper or the lower blade of a pair of scissors that cuts the piece of paper.

ALFRED MARSHALL
Economics of Industry, 1879

[304] It is often said that the modern forms of industrial life are distinguished from the earlier by being more competitive. But this account is not quite satisfactory. The strict meaning of competition seems to be the facing of one person against another, with special reference to bidding for the sale or purchase of anything. This kind of

facing is no doubt both more intense and more wisely extended than it used to be: but it is only a secondary, and one might almost say, an accidental consequence from the fundamental characteristics of modern life.

There is no one term that will express these characteristics adequately. They are . . . a certain independence and habit of choosing one's own course for oneself, a self-reliance; a deliberation and yet a promptness of choice and judgement, and a habit of forecasting the future and of shaping one's course with reference to distant aims.

ALFRED MARSHALL
Principles of Economics, 1890

[305] So vital to Britain's prosperity is the maintenance of full freedom for horizontal, rather than vertical expansion, that the country has a deep interest in defending the home market for everything that a manufacturer may desire to purchase, against an artificial manipulation of its prices by a cartel.

ALFRED MARSHALL
Industry and Trade, 1919

[306] If the Treasury were to fill old bottles with banknotes, bury them at suitable depths in disused coal-mines which are then filled up to the surface with town rubbish, and leave it to private enterprise on well-tried principles of *laissez-faire* to dig the notes up again (the right to do so being obtained, of course, by tendering the leases of the note-bearing territory), there need be no more unemployment and, with the help of the repercussions, the real income of the community, and its capital wealth also, would probably become a good deal greater than it actually is. It would, indeed, be more sensible to build houses and the like; but

if there are political and practical difficulties in the way of this, the above would be better than nothing.

JOHN MAYNARD KEYNES
The General Theory of Employment, Interest and Money, 1936

[307] The liberal argument is in favour of making the best possible use of the forces of competition as a means of co-ordinating human efforts, not an argument for leaving things just as they are. It is based on the conviction that where effective competition can be created, it is a better way of guiding individual efforts than any other. It does not deny, but even emphasizes, that, in order that competition should work beneficially, a carefully thought-out legal framework is required, and that neither the existing nor the past legal rules are free from grave defects. Nor does it deny that where it is impossible to create the conditions necessary to make competition effective, we must resort to other methods of guiding economic activity.

Economic liberation is opposed, however, to competition being supplanted by inferior methods of co-ordinating individual efforts. And it regards competition as superior not only because it is in most circumstances the most efficient method known, but even more because it is the only method by which our activities can be adjusted to each other without coercive or arbitrary intervention of authority. Indeed, one of the main arguments in favour of competition is that it dispenses with the need for 'conscious social control' and that it gives the individuals a chance to decide whether the prospects of a particular occupation are sufficient to compensate for the disadvantages and risks connected with it.

F. A. HAYEK
The Road to Serfdom, 1944

[308] If production creates the wants it seeks to satisfy, or if the wants emerge *pari passu* with the production, then the urgency of the wants can no longer be used to defend the urgency of the production. Production only fills a void that it has itself created. . . . Consumer wants can have bizarre, frivolous, or even immoral origins, and an admirable case can still be made for a society that seeks to satisfy them. But the case cannot stand if it is the process of satisfying wants that creates wants. For then the individual who urges the importance of production to satisfy these wants is precisely in the position of the onlooker who applauds the efforts of the squirrel to keep abreast of the wheel that is propelled by his own efforts.

JOHN KENNETH GALBRAITH
The Affluent Society, 1958

[309] Entrepreneurship is creativeness. It abhors the sacred cows as nature abhors a vacuum. It is always creating obsolescence of something. It is engaged in 'creative destruction'. If your company is not entrepreneurial, another one will be. And because of that entrepreneurship, your company will not live long enough to regret it. Therefore there should be no question as to whether your firm will pursue the course of the entrepreneur. It has no choice. . . . Creative destruction should be the rule of life.

THEODORE LEVITT
Innovation in Marketing, 1962

[310] It seems to the present writer that the moral to be drawn from capitalist experience is that production will never be responsive to consumer needs as long as the initiative lies with the producer. Even within capitalism consumers are beginning to organize to defend themselves. In a

planned economy the best hope seems to be to develop a class of functionaries, playing the role of wholesale dealers, whose career and self-respect depend upon satisfying the consumer. They could keep in touch with demand through the shops; market research, which in the capitalist world is directed to finding out how to bamboozle the housewife, could be directed to discovering what she really needs; design and quality could be imposed upon manufacturing enterprises and the product mix settled by placing orders in such a way as to hold a balance between economies of scale and variety of tastes.

No one who has lived in the capitalist world is deceived by the pretence that the market system ensures consumer's sovereignty. It is up to the socialist economies to find some way of giving it reality. JOAN ROBINSON

'Consumer's Sovereignty in a Planned Economy',
Collected Economic Papers, 1965

[311] The spirit of the monopolists is narrow, lazy, and oppressive: their work is more costly and less productive than that of independent artists; and the new improvements so eagerly grasped by the competition of freedom are admitted with slow and sullen reluctance in those proud corporations, above the fear of a rival, and below the confession of an error. EDWARD GIBBON

Autobiography, 1796

[312] It has to be recognized that a general abandonment of the assumption of perfect competition, a universal assumption of monopoly, must have very destructive consequences for economic theory. Under monopoly the stability conditions become indeterminate; and the basis on

which economic laws can be constructed is therefore shorn away. Not only is falling average cost consistent with monopoly; falling marginal cost is consistent with monopoly too. There must indeed be something to stop the indefinite expansion of the firm; but it can just as well be stopped by the limitation of the market as by rising marginal costs. . . .

SIR JOHN HICKS
Value and Capital, 1939

[313] It appears to me impossible but that the increase of intelligence, of education, and of love of independence among the working classes, must be attended with the corresponding growth of the good sense which manifests itself in provident habits of conduct, and that population, therefore, will bear a gradually diminishing ratio to capital and employment.

JOHN STUART MILL
Principles of Political Economy

[314] Certainly trivialities and vulgarities are now a greater proportion of our total output than in the past, not because taste has deteriorated—it probably was always bad—but because it is satisfied more often. Affluence changes the ability to satisfy taste rather than the taste: whereas in the past only the rich had the privilege to indulge their taste, now the poor can too. I do not see why transferring expenditures to a government no wiser than the voters who elect it and less able to satisfy *individual* tastes would solve this problem. It would probably replace private folly with official silliness. *Si monumentum quaeris, circumspice.* And it would make harder satisfaction of the minority tastes, which are usually more interesting than those of the majoirty.

ERNEST VAN DEN HAAG
'Private and Public Expenditures', *Modern Age*, Spring 1962

[315] No doubt there is great scope for educating taste; it is necessary to safeguard the interests of children; consumption of some commodities (motor cars, for instance) imposes external dis-economies on other consumers, and so forth. But, by and large, the freedom of the consumer to spend his money as he chooses may be accepted as the basis of the concept of a rational price system. JOAN ROBINSON

'Consumer's Sovereignty in a Planned Economy', *Collected Economic Papers*, 1965

[316] It is one of history's little ironies that these very same years are witnessing in the European Communist countries an enthusiastic and excited re-discovery and exploration of the market method of establishing economic tasks and allocating resources. . . . It is a useful reminder of the fact that adoption and maintenance of the market system for regulating the economic behaviour of citizens is itself an aspect of government. We in the West are accustomed to associate the market system with the ideas of personal liberty, freedom of the individual, and so forth; historically we see it as part of the nineteenth-century liberal creed. Yet its adoption in Eastern Europe owes nothing to such associations or theories, and is not felt to be inconsistent with the ethos and outlook of a Communist state. Whether the working of the market system will not itself produce other social and psychological changes inconsistent with a Communist régime, is a different question, and remains to be seen. J. ENOCH POWELL

How Big Should Government Be?, 1968

[317] Entrepreneurial decisions are largely technical or dependent on special knowledge and talent, so that it is very

misleading to draw a far-reaching analogy between political and economic life. Economic decisions cannot be efficiently taken by counting hands no matter how appropriate the political process may be for moral and political questions where orderly collective action depends primarily on consent. This proved to be so even in communist countries where the pressure of public opinion is increasingly being felt. 'Economic democracy' would seem to be as difficult to work as 'military democracy' or 'scientific democracy'.

LJUBO SIRC
Economic Devolution in Eastern Europe, 1969

[318] All argument in favour of free competition rests on one tacit assumption, which, however, corresponds but little to reality, namely that from the beginning all men are equal. If that were so, everyone would be equipped with the same working power, the same education and, above all, the same economic assets, and much could then be said in favour of free, unhampered competition; each person would have only himself to blame if he did not succeed.

But if all conditions are basically unequal, if some people have good hands from the beginning and others hold only low cards, free competition does nothing to stop the former from winning every trick while the latter pay the table.

KNUT WICKSELL
Quoted in the *Life* by T. Gardlund, 1958

[319] All business is in the nature of a game more or less difficult; and requires the same sort of faculties, and the same kind of attention, as a game. But in most trades a capitalist has to govern others; a large employer of labour has to govern many men. He has not only to move his pawns,

but to rule his pawns. The pieces with which he plays are of flesh and blood, and will not move unless they like. He has to manage that they shall like. And, unless he is paid for all this, the article will not be made. WALTER BAGEHOT
Economic Studies, 1888

[320] The term 'competition' has gathered about it an evil savour, and has come to imply a certain selfishness and indifference to the well-being of others. Now it is true that there is a less deliberate selfishness in early than in modern forms of industry; but there is also less deliberate unselfishness. It is deliberateness, and not selfishness, that is the characteristic of the modern age. . . .

We may conclude that the term 'competition' is not well suited to describe the special characteristics of industrial life in the modern age. We need a term that does not imply any moral qualities, whether good or evil, but which indicates the undisputed fact that modern business and industry are characterized by more self-reliant habits, more forethought, more deliberate and free choice, There is not any one term adequate for this purpose: but *Freedom of Industry and Enterprise*, or more shortly, *Economic Freedom*, points in the right direction. ALFRED MARSHALL
Principles of Economics, 1890

[321] Competition is the great enemy of economic privilege for a group. It can destroy groups altogether (as those founded on attempted monopolies) and it will maintain others (as those founded on human capacities) only for individuals whose contribution is regularly tested in the market and who are summarily ejected if found wanting. Instead of the spectacular massed battles between the

interests which have come to be staged in modern times with the deliberate intention of provoking government intervention, competition breaks up the campaign into petty and harmless squabbles on a thousand fronts.

A. S. J. BASTER
The Twilight of American Capitalism, 1937

[322] The view that an industry is a customer-satisfying process, not a goods-producing process, is vital for all businessmen to understand. An industry begins with the customer and his needs, not with a patent, a raw material, or a selling skill. Given the customer's needs, the industry develops backward, first concerning itself with the physical delivery of customer satisfactions. Then it moves back further to creating the things by which these satisfactions are in part achieved. How these materials are created is a matter of indifference to the customer; hence the particular form of manufacturing, processing, or what have you, cannot be considered as a vital aspect of the industry. Finally, the industry moves back still further to finding the raw materials necessary for making its products.

THEODORE LEVITT
Innovation in Marketing, 1962

[323] How can any rational man imagine that, as a matter of course, by increasing the manufacture of razors or scissors, he could increase their sales? That sale is pre-determined by the need; and, although undoubtedly a very slight need may come to operate as a great need when the price is suddenly or much lowered, yet *that* is merely a transitional effect; the lower price is probably *binomial* price, and binomial price cannot last; by its very nature it is a force tending to a

particular effect, viz. to equilibriate the supply with the demand, and, as soon as that tendency is accomplished, *there* it ceases. THOMAS DE QUINCEY

The Logic of Political Economy, 1844

[324] Successful planning is even more impossible where men have freedom to choose what they will buy, that is to say, freedom to determine what kind of life they will make for themselves out of the product of their labour. For then the planner must make guesses about the preferences of the people, and he might guess wrong. . . . Once a people has risen above the level of subsistence to the level where it has income to spend for comforts and luxuries, the caprices of individual taste become extremely disconcerting to the planning commissioners. WALTER LIPPMANN

The Method of Freedom, 1934

[325] The level of labour productivity is decisive for the consolidation and development of the new democratic system. The activists, in taking the lead in the struggle for the implementation of the great economic plan, have accomplished the greatest achievement in the consolidation of the democratic system and for the improvement of the life of our people. . . .

The great achievement of the activists in the last half of last year was that they succeeded in breaking through a vicious circle. With the aid of the initiative of the youth teams and the activists it became possible to increase production and thereby to prove that increasing labour productivity and raising agricultural yields can improve supplies to the people and the general living conditions.

What is needed now is to ensure that the workers should

overcome their old habits from the days of capitalism, when they had no interest in their work. Now that the nationally-owned enterprises are in the hands of the working people, the central aim must be to prove that the nationally-owned enterprises produce better, that labour productivity in these enterprises is higher than in private capitalist enterprises. WALTER ULBRICHT

Speech in East Berlin, 5 February 1949

[326] It is no use planning to produce more goods if you cannot sell them.

Here, stated in the simplest, common-sense, business man's language, we have an important principle that is too often neglected. It may, if preferred, be re-stated in more formal economic language by saying that a policy of promoting economic growth will be unsuccessful if the effect is to distort the allocation of productive resources (between industries) in relation to the markets available to them. It is quite true that an expansion of production does of itself generate additional purchasing power and additional demand. There are occasions, such as the 1930's, when it is clear that there has been an all-round failure of demand, and when almost anything that can be done to increase demand is therefore desirable. Too much of our economic thinking however still appears to take an over-simplified view of the problem, based upon the conditions of those times, that are not likely to recur. COLIN CLARK

Growthmanship, 1961

[327] One form of maladjustment which has been more experienced in the United States than in Britain is the

'temporary satiation' of wants. People in their struggle to keep up with the Jones's seem suddenly to get tired and decide to stay where they are. After a year or two their eagerness to compete with one another seems to return and the economy starts growing again. Too little is known about this 'temporary satiation' or about what causes it. Much more research needs to be done. In economic terminology the propensity to save voluntarily suddenly rises to a high level. In so far as this cannot be predicted beforehand, it means that manufacturers' production schedules are made to look too optimistic. RONALD BRECH

Britain 1984, 1963

[328] Economic progress is determined by technological advance, by private enterprise, and by what might be described as the perpetual plebiscite of the markets.

WALTER LIPPMANN

The Method of Freedom, 1934

[329] If effective demand is deficient, not only is the public scandal of wasted resources intolerable, but the individual enterpriser who seeks to bring these resources into action is operating with the odds loaded against him. The game of hazard which he plays is furnished with many zeros, so that the players *as a whole* will lose if they have the energy and hope to deal all the cards. Hitherto the increment of the world's wealth has fallen short of the aggregate of positive individual savings; and the difference has been made up by the losses of those whose courage and initiative have not been supplemented by exceptional skill or unusual good fortune. But if effective demand is adequate, average skill and average good fortune will be enough.

The authoritarian state systems of today seem to solve the problem of unemployment at the expense of efficiency and of freedom. It is certain that the world will not much longer tolerate the unemployment which, apart from brief intervals of excitement, is associated—and, in my opinion, inevitably associated—with present-day capitalistic individualism. But it may be possible by a right analysis of the problem of cure the disease whilst preserving efficiency and freedom. JOHN MAYNARD KEYNES

The General Theory of Employment, Interest and Money, 1936

[330] Every human being is a consumer, even if not a producer. Every improvement in the technique of manufacture means a potential increase in freedom of consumption. So does every increase in real wages. Hence a comparison of the real wages in different countries tells us a good deal about the amount of this kind of freedom. Given the possibility of buying something beyond essential food, clothing, and shelter, freedom depends on the choice of commodities or services which is available and the way in which the choice is actually made. J. B. S. HALDANE

A Comparative Study of Freedom, 1942

[331] An intellectual who is making a fairly good living often regards himself as almost absolutely free. He is freer than many of his fellows. But he is only free because his product, whether in science, art, or literature, happens to find a market. When the market changes he finds that his freedom may be freedom to starve. J. B. S. HALDANE

A Comparative Study of Freedom, 1942

[332] Obviously the company has to do what survival

demands. It has to adapt to the requirements of the market, and it has to do it sooner rather than later. But mere survival is a so-so aspiration. Anybody can survive in some way or other.... The trick is to survive gallantly, to feel the surging impulse of commercial mastery; not just to experience the sweet smell of success, but to have the visceral feel of entrepreneurial greatness. THEODORE LEVITT

Innovation in Marketing, 1962

[333] Can we conceive a time when man can no longer form even reasonable desires? Let us not forget that a desire which might be unreasonable in a former state of civilization—at a time when all the human faculties were absorbed in providing for low material wants—ceases to be so when improvement opens to these faculties a more extended field. A desire to travel at the rate of thirty miles an hour would have seemed unreasonable two centuries ago—it is not so at the present day. To pretend that the wants and desires of man are fixed and stationary quantities is to mistake the nature of the human soul, to deny facts, and to render civilization inexplicable. FREDERIC BASTIAT

Harmonies of Political Economy, 1860

[334] If the consumer cannot choose; if he must take what the producer offers; if the producer, whether a private producer or the state or a marketing department, is master of the market, instead of the consumer; then the situation must arise that the consumer serves, ultimately, as a kind of money supply and rubbish remover for the producer, instead of the producer serving the needs and desires of the consumer.

K. R. POPPER

The Open Society and Its Enemies, 1945

[335] It is a phenomenon well worthy of remark, how quickly, by continuous satisfaction, what was at first only a vague desire becomes a taste, and what was only a taste is transformed into a want, and even a want of the most imperious kind. FREDERIC BASTIAT
Harmonies of Political Economy, 1860

[336] If the concentration of marketing could be attained by methods that are free from cumbrous negotiations and effort, it would be a great social gain: for marketing is not wholly constructive work; and the less energy is devoted to it, the better for the general well-being. ALFRED MARSHALL
Industry and Trade, 1919

[337] Every conceivable alternative stands either above or below any other that you may select, or on a level with it. And the things so valued constitute the man's relative scale of preferences, the basis upon which his life is built. This scale of preferences is the register of the man's ideals, of the relative weight and value that he attaches to this or that alternative under every variety of condition. . . .

The man who can make his fellows desire more worthily and wisely is doubtless performing a higher task than the one who enables them more amply to satisfy whatever desires they have. The prophet and the poet may regenerate the world without the economist, but the economist cannot regenerate it without them. Yet he, too, has his place. He may help to guide if he cannot inspire. If he can give no strength he may save strength from being wasted. It is his misery that he cannot glorify the purposes to which he ministers, but it is his triumph that he can be glorified by them. He works in faith, for he knows that his work is barren unless others greater than he are working too, but he believes that wherever they are he can serve them. If he can give sight to some blind reforming Samson he too has served.

PHILIP H. WICKSTEED
The Common Sense of Political Economy, 1910

[338] Among the declarations of faith in the future is the act of buying. Each time we go out and buy a new car or decide to purchase a new suit, a pair of shoes, a house, we base our decision on a philosophy of life, a *Weltanschauung*. Buying is more than a commercial function. It deserves scientific study without moral judgement.

ERNEST DICHTER
The Strategy of Desire, 1960

[339] I am . . . concerned to show how, in this larger context of change, the forces inducing human effort have changed. This assaults not merely the most majestic of all economic assumptions, namely that man in his economic activities is subject to the authority of the market. Instead, we have an economic system which, whatever its formal ideological billing, is in substantial part a planned economy. The initiative in deciding what is to be produced comes not from the sovereign consumer who, through the market, issues the instructions that bend the productive mechanism to his ultimate will. Rather it comes from the great producing organization which reaches forward to control the markets that it is presumed to serve and, beyond, to bend the consumer to its needs.

JOHN KENNETH GALBRAITH
The New Industrial State, 1967

[340] Galbraith has his finger on something real, but he misses the strategic point. Mass production does indeed

generate great pressure to 'move' the product. But what usually gets emphasized is selling, not marketing. Marketing, being a more sophisticated and complex process, gets ignored.

The difference between marketing and selling is more than semantic. Selling focuses on the needs of the seller, marketing on the needs of the buyer. Selling is preoccupied with the seller's need to convert his product into cash; marketing with the idea of satisfying the needs of customer by means of the product and the whole cluster of things associated with creating, delivering, and finally consuming it.

THEODORE LEVITT
'Marketing Myopia', *Harvard Business Review*, 1960

[341] A productive system . . . may be conceived as a process of response to a continuous general election on the principle of proportional representation. The entrepreneur may, so to speak, put up the candidates; he may attempt to sway the election by propaganda and persuasion; but the ultimate decision lies with those who spend—with what is sometimes called the sovereignty of the consumer.

LORD ROBBINS
Politics and Economics, 1963

[342] In many cases, though not in all, the capitalist must make known the goodness—or, at least, must allege the goodness—of his own work. Advertising is a kind of outlay which to some extent is essential in all trades, and it takes different forms. A company which hires a showy shop front, a broker who is for ever sending round trade circulars, are really advertising just as much as dealers who insert in the newspapers puffs of their articles: the end in all cases is to

sell something, and in the long run the buyer pays for it all.

WALTER BAGEHOT
Economic Studies, 1879

[343] It is quite obvious that the price paid by the consumer includes marketing costs, which to a varying, but to a large, extent are expenses not of supplying the goods but of supplying them under conditions involving the expense of advertisement and competitive distribution.

R. H. TAWNEY
The Acquisitive Society, 1921

[344] Professional advertising men, who . . . have wished for a substantial social justification for their services, have frequently argued that without their efforts to stimulate wants men would not work and the economy would falter. Economists, almost without exception, have dismissed this as the special pleading of an economically unlearned and conscience-ridden community. In fact, the advertising men have a good case. It has been rejected by economists because to admit that advertising promotes wants is to concede that the goods would be unwanted in the absence of such persuasion. This casts doubt on the pivotal contentions that wants are homogeneous and insatiable and that the volume of production measures the success of the society. One cannot give equal status with bread to what must be contrived by advertising and one cannot measure the success of an economy by its ability to keep up with Madison Avenue.

JOHN KENNETH GALBRAITH
Footnote in *The New Industrial State*, 1967

[345] Competition in falsehood ultimately discredits all advertisement.

H. G. WELLS
The Work, Wealth and Happiness of Mankind, 1932

[346] No reputable manufacturer wants to sell his goods on false or misleading information. Even if he did, he would not stay long in business; the public are not fools, and the proverb that honesty is the best policy is a very sound one. Indeed, if the manufacturers who advertise in the columns of my newspapers and magazines, and on my radio and television stations, attempted to mislead the buying public in the way in which some politicians and publicists attempt to mislead the electorate, they would very soon find themselves in goal. LORD THOMSON OF FLEET

'Advertising and the Public Interest', *The Advertising Quarterly*, 1964

[347] A mixture of a lie doth ever add pleasure. Doth any man doubt, that if there were taken out of men's minds vain opinions, flattering hopes, false valuations, imaginations . . . and the like, but it would leave the minds of men poor shrunken things, full of melancholy and indisposition, and unpleasing to themselves. FRANCIS BACON

On Truth, 1597

[348] Commerce has passed the sordid age, and just as the Government employs a St Gaudens to beautify its coins, so the world of business is making its appeal to the wit, imagination and artistic sense of the people.

J. WALTER THOMPSON

1907

[349] Advertising is social action, produced by society and limited by it. But there is another aspect of social action to be considered, the fact that few, or no, kinds of social behaviour produce only the results that are intended. If we define social action as human behaviour which is intended to influence the behaviour of others, then one of the paradoxes

of advertising is that its direct influence in almost every case cannot be precisely assessed, and may even be zero or negative, but that, in general, and along with other elements of the social fabric, its indirect effects are, and presumably will go on being, very considerable. Advertising, in fact, affects its own market in unintended, important, and under-estimated ways. DONALD MACRAE

'Advertising and Social Structure', *The Advertising Quarterly*, 1964

[350] Advertising is to me the outward and visible sign of the whole absurdity of our present way of life. So much wealth, so much talent going into persuading people to want what they don't want to use what they don't need to consume what makes them sick. And this at a time when the greater part of mankind is falling into ever greater destitution.

MALCOLM MUGGERIDGE

The Times, June 1966

[351] Advertising is called upon not only to speed up the marketing of commodities, but also to educate the purchaser and develop his taste, and hence the demand as well. It popularizes the most efficient ways of using commodities and helps to improve trade. YAKOV ORLOV

Editor, 'Sovietkaya Torgovia', *The Financial Times*, June 1966

[352] We should spare no effort in the organization of good advertising. Neither should we economize on advertising, because money spent on it is repaid a hundredfold.

A. ARGUNOV

Journal of the Soviet Ministry of Trade, February 1966

[353] A market need not be perfect in order to be superior to no market at all. All competition in the real world is

imperfect but, however imperfect it is, it will still tend to a more effective employment of resources than would be achieved in its absence. . . .

There can be no worse unfairness than to deny people the chance to put whatever assets they have to what they judge the best use. The market is the fairest standard, impartial and impersonal, treating like things alike, which is in the essence of justice. J. ENOCH POWELL

Saving in a Free Society, 1960

[354] Innovations in the economic system do not as a rule take place in such a way that first new wants arise spontaneously in consumers and then the productive apparatus swings round through their pressure. . . . It is . . . the producer who as a rule initiates economic change, and consumers are educated by him if necessary; they are, as it were, taught to want new things, or things which differ in some respect or other from those which they have been in the habit of using. J. A. SCHUMPETER

The Theory of Economic Development, 1911

[355] I sometimes think that the chief danger to the prestige of the price system comes from its tepid friends. They argue that, of course, free markets are good for rich countries, but not for poor. In the poor countries the state must take a very active hand. But even with the rich countries, they must not get too rich because then they become affluent and consumers will not know how to spend their money and the state, once again, according to this argument, must take a bigger hand. The price system, it is said, may be good in more tranquil times when prices are not changing much, but no good in storm-tossed times for then price

movements will not bring about the required adjustments quickly enough. Once again, the tranquil times must not be too tranquil because that will be evidence that evil monopolists or oligopolists or monopsonists are on the prowl. So when the tepid friends of free markets have made full allowance for all these exceptions, there is not really very much left of what they started with. JOHN JEWKES
In *Economics, Business and Government*, 1966

[356] Thus the paradox. The economy for its success requires organized public bamboozlement. At the same time it nurtures a growing class which feels itself superior to such bamboozlement and deplores it as intellectually corrupt. The subculture which requires such obfuscation for its existence can only be regarded with disdain. That culture responds with a sense of hurt and guilt and the indignation which comes from the knowledge that its needs sustain and nourish its academic critics. JOHN KENNETH GALBRAITH
The New Industrial State, 1967

[357] Many people set up in a city as merchants or undertakers, to buy the country produce from those who bring it or to order it to be brought on their account. They pay a certain price following that of the place where they purchase it, to resell wholesale or retail at an uncertain price.

Such undertakers are the wholesalers in wool and corn, bakers, butchers, manufacturers and merchants of all kinds who buy country produce and materials to work them up and resell them gradually as the inhabitants require them.

These undertakers can never know how great will be the demand in their city, nor how long their customers will buy of them since their rivals will try all sorts of means to attract customers from them. All this causes so much uncertainty among these undertakers that every day one sees some of them become bankrupt.

The manufacturer who has bought wool from the merchant or direct from the farmer cannot foretell the profit he will make in selling his cloths and stuffs to the merchant taylor. If the latter have not a reasonable sale he will not load himself with the cloths and stuffs of the manufacturer, especially if those stuffs cease to be in the fashion.

RICHARD CANTILLON
Essai sur la Nature du Commerce en Général, 1755

[358] An article is worth what it is worth, when and where it is wanted.

Christmas cracker motto, 1968

[359] Important as the moral influences of the market place are, they have not been subjected to any real study. The immense proliferation of general education, of scientific progress, and of democracy, are all coincidental in time and place with the emergence of the free enterprise system of organizing the market place. I believe this coincidence was not accidental. The economic progress of the past three centuries was both cause and effect of this general growth of freedom. The dominant era of the free market place was in the nineteenth century. I believe, but with less confidence, that the absence of major wars in that century—the only peaceable century in history—was related to this reign of liberty. I believe, again with less confidence, that the contemporary transformation of the British public from a violent and unruly people into a population of almost painful Victorian rectitude was related to this reign of liberty.

These beliefs may be right or wrong, but they are not matters of taste. They are hypotheses concerning the relationship between economic and social organization, and are subject to analytical development and empirical testing. It is time that we did so, high time. Our ruling attitude toward the market place has not changed since the time of Plato.

GEORGE J. STIGLER
The Intellectual and the Market Place, 1963

[360] Only professional defenders of the free enterprise system, members of a lowly and poorly paid craft, still argue for the rule of competition, this being the test their clients are best calculated to fail.

J. K. GALBRAITH
The New Industrial State, 1967

[361] There was . . . a great difference between the competition admired by orthodox economists and the struggle for existence which Darwin proclaimed as the motive force of evolution. 'Free competition' in orthodox economies is a very artificial conception, hedged in by legal restrictions. You may undersell a competitor, but you must not murder him. You must not use the armed forces of the State to help you to get the better of foreign manufacturers. Those who have not the good fortune to possess capital must not seek to improve their lot by revolution. 'Free competition', as understood by the Benthamites, was by no means really free.

BERTRAND RUSSELL
A History of Western Philosophy, 1946

[362] According to Adam Smith, society is a commercial enterprise. Every one of its members is a salesman. It is

evident how political economy establishes an *alienated* form of social intercourse as the *true and original* form, and that which corresponds to human nature.

The less you eat, drink and read books; the less you go to the theatre, the dance-hall, the public-house, the less you think, love, theorize, sing, paint, fence, etc., the more you save—the greater becomes your treasure which neither moths nor rust will devour, your capital. The less you are, the more you have; the less you express your own life, the greater is your *externalized* life—the greater is the store of your alienated being. Everything that the political economist takes from you in life and in humanity, he replaces for you in money and in wealth; and all the things that you cannot do, your money can do. KARL MARX

Marx-Engels Gesamensgabe. Quoted in *Adam Smith* by E. G. West, 1969

[363] Who says the utilities have no competition? They may be natural monopolies now, but tomorrow they may be natural deaths. To avoid this prospect, they too will have to develop fuel cells, solar energy, and other power sources. To survive, they themselves will have to plot the obsolescence of what now produces their livelihood.

THEODORE LEVITT

'Marketing Myopia', *Harvard Business Review*, 1960

[364] So long as effective freedom of exchange is maintained, the central feature of the market organization of economic activity is that it prevents one person from interfering with another in respect of most of his activities. The consumer is protected from coercion by the seller because of the presence of other sellers with whom he can deal. The seller is protected from coercion by the consumer because of

other consumers to whom he can sell. The employee is protected from coercion by the employer because of other employers for whom he can work, and so on. And the market does this impersonally and without centralized authority.

Indeed, a major source of objection to a free economy is precisely that it does this task so well. It gives people what they want instead of what a particular group thinks they ought to want. Underlying most arguments against the free market is a lack of belief in freedom itself.

The existence of a free market does not of course eliminate the need for government. On the contrary, government is essential both as a forum for determining the 'rules of the game' and as an umpire to interpret and enforce the rules decided on. What the market does is to reduce greatly the range of issues that must be decided through political means, and thereby to minimize the extent to which government need participate directly in the game.

MILTON FRIEDMAN
Capitalism and Freedom, 1962

[365] It is impossible for the authorities to gauge individual preferences. If a particular poor man has a great love for a certain type of article, he will save up for it and outbid a richer man.

Looking at the matter just a little more broadly, one sees that it is not true that the poor man has less to gain from the free working of the price mechanism than the rich. The reverse is true. What is the alternative? Arbitrary cuts in various items of consumption by the authority.

Now if circumstances give rise to some reduction in the national standard of living, say one of 10 per cent, for whom is the need greater to have freedom and to make the cut in his own expenditure just where it hurst him least? Clearly for the poor man. If the adjustment is made for him . . . by rationed allocation, this may amount not merely to imposing hardship, but to downright brutality. . . . If people must go without, let them at least choose what they will go without.

ROY HARROD
Are These Hardships Necessary?, 1947

[366] For particular products of firms, the forecasts of what is possible in five or ten years' time do not have the accuracy of the forecasts of the national income as a whole. This is a perfectly simple triusm but it is lost sight of. If you aim to produce the detailed requirements built up into the aggregate, your detailed aims will be wrong because it is absolutely essential in a competitive economy to be flexible and to change your targets as consumer demand or technology changes, both in Britain and overseas. Therefore, we should not have our eye on what is to be produced in five or ten years' time, but on what the market is going to want in five or ten years' time. As markets change perhaps every year or two, we have to change our plans, and only by watching profitability are these changes likely to be spotted in time and the necessary action taken. If you are working to a national plan, which is inevitably static, your objectives will be the wrong objectives, and that is a serious danger in Britain today. Working towards a fixed target is not only dangerous but self-destructive if your purpose is progress.

SIR PAUL CHAMBERS
In *Economics, Business and Government*, 1966

[367] The presence or absence of a price system is not proof of anything. For the price system, in itself, is a neutral though

powerful weapon. A knife may be used for social purposes, like peeling potatoes, or anti-social purposes, like cutting other people's throats. So, too, the value of a price system for the purpose of increasing economic welfare lies in the environment in which it is allowed to operate. If it is allowed freely to direct producers to the goods most needed and consumers to the goods which provide the greatest satisfaction, for the minimum of effort, it is doing its job properly. But, of course, a price system can be manipulated for bringing about the most evil ends: for the destruction of a social group, for the starvation of a whole community, for the gratification of the sadistic influences of one man. Or it may, through sheer ignorance, be so mishandled as to produce spectacular and unnecessary shortages of goods—as the price-control system in Great Britain and the United States did after the war.

JOHN JEWKES
The New Ordeal by Planning, 1968

VII

The Planned Society

[368] The State exists not merely to make life possible but to make life good.

ARISTOTLE
c. 340 B.C.

[369] We consider a man who takes no interest in the State not as harmless, but as useless; and although only a few may originate a policy, we are all able to judge it.

PERICLES OF ATHENS
c. 430 B.C. From the Funeral Oration

[370] The situation in the Roman Empire was in effect novel. Pericles had conceived a freedom for private actions, of a certain civilized type within narrowly restricted bounds. Plato voices the claim for contemplative freedom. But the Empire was faced with the claim for freedom of corporate action. Modern political history, from that day to this, is the confused story of the strenuous resistance of the State, and of its partial concessions.

ALFRED NORTH WHITEHEAD
Adventures of Ideas, 1933

[371] I have observed that wealthy nations have need of hospitals, because fortune subjects them to a thousand accidents; but it is plain that transient assistances are much better than foundations. The evil is momentary; it is necessary, therefore, that the succour should be of the same nature, and that it be applied to particular accidents.

MONTESQUIEU
The Spirit of the Laws, 1748

[372] He had not imagined that in a kingdom subject to one and the same prince, all the towns would regard each other as enemies, would arrogate to themselves the right of preventing Frenchmen called foreigners from working inside their

own boundary, of opposing the sale and free passage of the commodities of a neighbouring province and of thus fighting, for the sake of a trifling interest, the general interest of the State. . . .

He was no less astonished to see the Government occupy itself with regulating the price of each commodity, proscribing one kind of industry in order by that to make another flourish; putting particular hindrances in the way of sales of the provisions which are most necessary for life; prohibiting the accumulation of stores of a thing of which the harvest varies every year while its consumption is always much the same; prohibiting the export of a thing subject to extreme depressions of price, and fancying that it ensured abundance of corn by making the condition of the cultivator more uncertain and unhappy than that of all other citizens. ANNE ROBERT JACQUES TURGOT

Elogé de Gournay, 1770

[373] All government—indeed, every human benefit and enjoyment, every virtue and every prudent act—is founded on compromise and barter. EDMUND BURKE

Speech on the Conciliation with America, 1775

[374] The sovereign has . . . the duty of erecting and maintaining certain public works and certain public institutions which it never can be for the interest of any individual or small group of individuals, to erect and maintain; because the profit could never repay the expense . . . though it may frequently do much more than repay it to a great society.

ADAM SMITH

The Wealth of Nations, 1776

[375] The day will come when this country will shudder at its

tolerance of that state of things when it was rolling in wealth. . . . In so far as poverty is due to conditions over which man has no control, then the State should step in to the very utmost of its resources. LLOYD GEORGE

In a speech at Swansea, 1908

[376] Everywhere the State acquires more and more direct control over the humblest members of the community, and a more exclusive power of governing each of them in his smallest concerns. . . . Diversity, as well as freedom, is disappearing day by day. ALEXIS DE TOCQUEVILLE

Democracy in America, 1835

[377] Socialism has two elements: the frenzy of contradiction, and the madness of pride. FREDERIC BASTIAT

Harmonies of Political Economy, 1845

[378] When the service becomes public, all individual roles of conduct and action disappear, and are mixed up and generalized in a written, coercive and inflexible law, which is the same for all, which makes no allowance for particular situations, and strikes the noblest faculties of human nature with numbness and torpor. FREDERIC BASTIAT

Harmonies of Political Economy, 1845

[379] Government aid . . . should be so given as to be as far as possible a course of education for the people in the art of accomplishing great objects by individual energy and voluntary co-operation. JOHN STUART MILL

Principles of Political Economy, 1848

[380] Man cannot live in the midst of plenty. All cannot share

alike the bounties of nature. Were there no established administration of property, every man would be obliged to guard with force his little store. Selfishness would be triumphant. The subjects of contention would be perpetual. Every individual would be under a constant anxiety about corporal support, and not a single intellect would be left free to expatiate in the field of thought.

THOMAS ROBERT MALTHUS
An Essay on the Principle of Population (1798). 6th edn., 1826

[381] The question is whether (under Communism) there would be any asylum left for individuality of character; whether public opinion would not be a tyrannical yoke; whether the absolute dependence of each on all, the surveillance of each by all, would not grind down into a tame uniformity of thoughts, feelings and actions. This is already one of the glaring evils of the existing state of Society, notwithstanding a much greater diversity of education and pursuits and a much less absolute dependence of the individual on the mass, than would exist in a Communist régime. No Society in which eccentricity is a matter of reproach, can be in a wholesome state. It has yet to be ascertained whether the Communistic scheme would be favourable to the multiform development of human nature.

JOHN STUART MILL
Principles of Political Economy, 1848

[382] The socialists . . . forget that wherever competition is not, monopoly is, and that monopoly, in all its forms, is the taxation of the industrious for the support of indolence, if not of plunder.

JOHN STUART MILL
Principles of Political Economy, 1848

[383] Even plunder or confiscation is less fatal to abstinence than what is called socialism or communism. The first only incidentally diminish the motives to production, the second aims specifically at destroying them. It proposes to enact that industry shall not be rewarded by wages nor abstinence by profit; that those who toil shall toil for others and those who save shall save for others—in short, that hope shall cease to govern mankind. If this system should ever be attempted or adopted. . . . it will be necessary to substitute fear, and the socialist nation, unless it is to starve, must be divided into slaves and slave drivers.

NASSAU WILLIAM SENIOR
Oxford Lectures, 1848–49

[384] The worth of a State, in the long run, is the worth of the individuals composing it; and a State which postpones the interests of *their* mental expansion and elevation, to a little more administrative skill, or of that semblance of it which practice gives, in the details of business; a State which dwarfs its men, in order that they may be more docile instruments in its hands even for beneficial purposes—will find that with small men no great thing can really be accomplished; and that the perfection of machinery to which it has sacrificed everything, will in the end avail it nothing, for want of the vital power which, in order that the machine might work more smoothly, it has preferred to banish.

JOHN STUART MILL
On Liberty, 1859

[385] If the roads, the railways, the banks, the insurance offices, the great joint stock companies, the universities, and the public charities, were all of them branches of the

government; if, in addition, the municipal corporations and local boards, with all that now devolves on them, became departments of the central administration; if the employees of all these different enterprises were appointed and paid by the government, and looked to the government for every rise in life; not all the freedom of the press and popular constitution of the legislature would make this or any other country free otherwise than in name. And the evil would be greater, the more efficiently and scientifically the administrative machinery were constructed—the more skilful the arrangements for obtaining the best qualified hands and heads with which to work it.

JOHN STUART MILL
On Liberty, 1859

[386] Socialism, like any decent creed, may be a means of making a man behave better than he would without it; but it is no guarantee of good behaviour. G. D. H. COLE
Economic Tracts for the Times, 1932

[387] In an economy which is directed according to a plan and for definite national objectives, the official must be superior to the citizen. . . . The citizen is a conscript; in principle his life is dedicated to the State, in practice it is dedicated to the officials who issue his order to him.

WALTER LIPPMANN
The Method of Freedom, 1934

[388] The State should do for the people what needs to be done, but which they cannot, by individual effort, do at all, or do as well for themselves. ABRAHAM LINCOLN
1860

[389] The most important *Agenda* of the State relate not to those activities which private individuals are already fulfilling, but to those functions which fall outside the sphere of the individual, to those decisions which are made by *no one* if the State does not make them. The important thing for Government is not to do things which individuals are doing already, and to do them a little better or a little worse; but to do those things which at present are not done at all.

JOHN MAYNARD KEYNES
The End of Laissez-Faire, 1926

[390] A study of the history of the French Revolution will show that it was carried on precisely in that same spirit which has caused so many abstract books to be written on government. There was the same attraction towards general theories, complete systems of legislation, and exact symmetry in the laws—the same contempt of existing facts—the same reliance upon theory—the same love of the original, the ingenious, and the novel in institutions—the same desire to reconstruct, all at once, the entire constitution by the rules of logic, and upon a single plan, rather than seek to amend it in its parts.

ALEXIS DE TOCQUEVILLE
On the State of Society in France before the Revolution of 1789, trans. 1873

[391] If the State is to be summoned not only to provide houses for the labouring classes, but also to supply such dwellings at nominal rents, it will, while doing something on behalf of their physical condition, utterly destroy their moral energies. It will, in fact, be an official proclamation that, without any efforts of their own, certain portions of the people shall enter into the enjoyment of many good things, altogether at the expense of others. The State is bound, in

such a case as this, to give every facility by law and enabling statutes; but the work itself should be founded, and proceed, on voluntary effort, for which there is in the country an adequate amount of wealth, zeal and intelligence.

. . . Should private bounty and private zeal be insufficient for the great issue now sought, it might then be necessary for the Government to interpose, and use the money of the State for the improvement of the domiciliary conditions of some portions of the labouring classes by placing them in new homes at eleemosynary rents; but such interposition must not take place until every effort has been made, every expedient exhausted, and indisputable proof given that, if the State does not do the work, it will never be done at all.

THE EARL OF SHAFTESBURY
'The Dwellings of the Poor', *The Nineteenth Century*, 1883

[392] Rents, wages, contracts—all the relations between man and man—must be matters of State interference. The existence of any matter not directly regulated by statute is a direct challenge to make one. VISCOUNT BURY
'The Unity of the Empire', *The Nineteenth Century*, 1885

[393] That State action always has been more or less misdirected, and always will be so, is, I believe, perfectly true. But I am not aware that it is more true of the action of men in their corporate capacity than it is of the doings of individuals. The wisest and most dispassionate man in existence, merely wishing to go from one stile in a field to the opposite, will not walk quite straight—he is always going a little wrong, and always correcting himself; and I can only congratulate the individualist who is able to say that his general course of life has been of a less undulating

character. To abolish State action, because its direction is never more than approximately correct, appears to me to be much the same thing as abolishing the man at the wheel altogether, because, do what he will, the ship yaws more or less. 'Why should I be robbed of my property to pay for teaching another man's children?' is an individualist question, which is not infrequently put as if it settled the whole business. Perhaps it does, but I find difficulties in seeing why it should. The parish in which I live makes me pay my share for the paving and lighting of a great many streets that I never pass through; and I might plead that I am robbed to smooth the way and lighten the darkness of other people. But I am afraid the parochial authorities would not let me off on this plea; and I must confess I do not see why they should.

T. H. HUXLEY
The Struggle for Existence, 1888

[394] If the State attempts to fulfil its engagement by itself giving work, it becomes itself a great employer of labour. As it is the only capitalist that cannot refuse employment, and as it is the capitalist whose workpeople are always the most lightly tasked, it will soon become the greatest, and soon after that the only great, employer, The public revenue, instead of merely supporting the government, will have to support all the industry of the country. As rents and profits are swallowed up by taxes, private property, now become a mere encumbrance, will be abandoned to the State; and subject to the duty of maintaining the people, the government will be the only proprietor. This is Communism.

If, on the other hand, the State, in order to escape from this train of consequences, does not find itself work but takes care that it shall always be supplied by individual capitalists, it must take care that at no place and at no time there be a stagnation. It must take on itself the management of both capitalists and labourers. It must see that the one class do not injure the other by over trading, or by competition. It must regulate profits and wages—sometimes retard, sometimes accelerate, production or consumption. In short .... it must organize industry. This is Socialism.

NASSAU WILLIAM SENIOR
Journals, 1871

[395] The collective ownership of the means of production would deaden the energies of mankind, and arrest economic progress; unless before its introduction the whole people had acquired a power of unselfish devotion to the public good which is now relatively rare. And . . . it might probably destroy much that is most beautiful and joyful in the private and domestic relations of life. These are the main reasons which cause patient students of economics generally to anticipate little good and much evil from schemes for sudden and violent reorganization of the economic, social and political conditions of life.

ALFRED MARSHALL
Principles of Economics, 1890

[396] Socialism, which has the future of the world in its hands, will probably be unable to abolish war, and will certainly not care for beauty or seek to preserve it. The reconstruction of society which Socialism contemplates will not be a state of things in which the beauty of either nature or art will be found and cherished. Collectivism must of necessity be colourless; equality can afford none of those heights and depths, those lights and shades, which are the essential charm of life as a landscape. When all the arable

earth is one huge allotment-ground a Corot will find no subject for his canvas, not even in his dreams, for his dreams will be dead of inanition. There can be I think no hope that this loss of beauty will not be greater and greater with every year. The tendency, continually increasing in the modern character, is to regard beauty and nature with cynical indifference, stirred, when stirred at all, into active insolence; such insolence as was expressed in the joke of the Chicago citizen who called the plank walls of his city 'the re-afforesting of our town'. It is a temper not merely brutal, but with a leer in it, which is more offensive than its brutality. OUIDA

'The Ugliness of Modern Life', *The Nineteenth Century*, 1896

[397] We cannot imagine a democracy, even a proletarian democracy, without representative institutions; but we can and must bring it into being without the parliamentary system, unless our criticism of bourgeois society is but empty words. LENIN

The State and Revolution, 1917

[398] Karl Marx would have denounced attempts at economic organization on national lines as *kleinburgerlich*—the peddling inventions of a bourgeois mentality that was not even abreast of the times. LIONEL ROBBINS

The Economic Basis of Class Conflict, 1939

[399] Our life in Russia is made up of the most striking contrasts—in economics as well as in everything else. In the very centre of the country, close to Moscow, there are miles of swamps, of impassable roads—and close by you might suddenly see a factory which would impress a European or American engineer by its technical equipment.

Similar contrasts abound in our national life. Side by side with some old-time type of domineering, rapacious profiteer, who has come to life again in the present generation, who has passed through revolution and expropriation, engaged in swindling and in masked and legalized profiteering, preserving intact all the while his suburban vulgarity and greediness—we see the best type of Communists of the working class who devote their lives day by day to the interests of the world's proletariat and are ready to fight at any given moment for the cause of the revolution in any country, even one they would be unable perhaps to locate on the map.

In addition to such social contrasts—obtuse bestiality and the highest revolutionary idealism—we often witness psychological contrasts in the same mind. A man is a sound Communist, devoted to the cause, but women are for him just 'females', not to be taken seriously in any way. Or it happens that a very deserving Communist, when discussing the smaller nationalities, starts talking hopelessly reactionary stuff. To account for that we must remember that different parts of the human consciousness do not change and develop simultaneously and on parallel lines.

There is a certain economy in the process. Human psychology is very conservative by nature, and the change due to the demands and the push of life affects, in the first place, those parts of the mind which are directly concerned in the case.

LEON TROTSKY
Problems of Everyday Life, 1923

[400] The Communist way of life will not form itself blindly, like coral islands, but will be built consciously, will be tested by thought, will be directed and corrected. Life

will cease to be elemental and, for this reason, stagnant. Man will learn to move rivers and mountains, to build peoples' palaces on the peaks of Mont Blanc and at the bottom of the Atlantic; and he will not only be able to impart richness, brilliancy, and intensity to his life but also the highest dynamic quality. The shell of life will hardly have time to form before it will burst open again under the pressure of new technical and cultural inventions and achievements. Life in the future will not be monotonous. LEON TROTSKY

Literature and Revolution, 1925

[401] I can quite conceive that in a Socialist future any attempt to obtain an economic advantage over one's neighbours, as distinguished from one an economic advantage for the whole community, might come to be considered such exceedingly bad form that nobody could make it without losing her place is society just as a detected card-sharper does at present. BERNARD SHAW

The Intelligent Woman's Guide to Socialism and Capitalism, 1928

[402] Would you ever have supposed from reading the newspapers that Communism, instead of being a wicked invention of Russian revolutionaries and British and American desperadoes, is a highly respectable way of sharing our wealth, sanctioned and practised by the apostles, and an indispensable part of our own daily life and civilization? The more Communism, the more civilization.

BERNARD SHAW

The Intelligent Woman's Guide to Socialism and Capitalism, 1928

[403] There is too much civilization, too much means of subsistence, too much industry, too much commerce. The productive forces at the disposal of society no longer tend to

further the development of the conditions of bourgeois property; on the contrary, they have become too powerful for these conditions, by which they are fettered, and so soon as they overcome these fetters, they bring disorder into the whole of bourgeois society, endanger the existence of bourgeois property. The conditions of bourgeois society are too narrow to comprise the wealth created by them. And how does the bourgeoisie get over these crises? On the one hand, by enforced destruction of a mass of productive forces; on the other, by the conquest of new markets, and by the more thorough exploitation of the old ones. That is to say, by paving the way for more extensive and more destructive crises, and by diminishing the means whereby crises are prevented. KARL MARX

Communist Manifesto, 1848

[404] As long as capitalism and Socialism remain, we cannot live in peace. In the end one or the other will triumph—a funeral requiem will be sung either over the Soviet Republic or over world capitalism. This is a respite in war. LENIN

Collected Works, 1929

[405] In the past we have not infrequently had to wait for a war to terminate a major depression. I hope that in future we shall not adhere to this purist financial attitude, and that we shall be ready to spend on the enterprises of peace what the financial maxims of the past only allow us to spend on the devastations of war. JOHN MAYNARD KEYNES

The World's Economic Crisis, 1932

[406] The people who talk of planning are not usually Socialists. They are trying to live in a half-way house

between capitalism and socialism. . . . I do not feel certain that this half-way house can stand.

SIR WILLIAM BEVERIDGE
The World's Economic Crisis, 1932

[407] 'I see what you are driving at. I knew it from the first. Centralization. No. Never with my consent. Not English.'

CHARLES DICKENS
Mr Podsnap in *Our Mutual Friend*, 1865

[408] Capitalism has become so complicated that private initiative is insufficient to regulate it; the democratization of political fore, a new view of the state and of economic order. The novelty is not that there is government intervention. That there has always been. Of that there might have been much more without marking any decisive change. The novelty is that the state is now compelled to look upon the economy as a national establishment for which it is responsible and not as a mere congerie of separate interests which it serves, protects, and regulates.

WALTER LIPPMANN
The Method of Freedom, 1934

[409] For the greater part of modern history, protective tariffs have made the world poorer than it would have been otherwise, without choking trade altogether. But when it is multiplied indefinitely—when on all sides you see the multiplication of restrictions on trade and investment—the erection of state-aided monopolies, and the limitations of free enterprise, then I submit you do not need to ask further why the phenomenon of poverty in the midst of plenty persists, or why, on any clear view of the future, it is likely to persist.

LIONEL ROBBINS
'The Twofold Roots of the Great Depression',
in *The Burden of Plenty?*, 1935

[410] Economic planning ought to be done at least on the national scale: that there should be some body of nation-wide authority charged with the duty of constructing a plan for the whole country, or at least with the duty of reviewing all our partial plans—plans for housing, plans for the relief of distressed areas, agricultural marketing plans, and so on—so as to make sure that they fit together, and that it is the public, and not merely sectional interests, that they are built to serve; and to ensure above all that we never forget that plenty is a fine thing, and that to attempt to suppress it is a most miserable confession of failure.

BARBARA WOOTTON
'The Necessity of Planning', in *The Burden of Plenty?*, 1935

[411] If a Planned Economy is adopted it will be a set Plan. It must not be departed from. . . . Anyone, worker or manager, who does not come up to schedule, lets down his bit of production, lets down all the others, the whole community. He becomes guilty of sabotage and must suffer a penalty. The Plan *must* be adhered to. And that means, too, that the Planners decide what consumers must consume, and how much.

GRAHAM HUTTON
The Burden of Plenty?, 1935

[412] In the Caucus-race in *Alice in Wonderland* . . . the Dodo took the prizes from Alice herself. Alice is the State; she has provided the prizes for everybody. Does she get one for herself, though? Well, in the book, the Dodo told her to hand over her own thimble, and then presented it back to her as a prize. That is roughly the position of the State today. It is expected by political parties and economic interests not

only to furnish everybody's prizes, but also to furnish its own prizes too. Can such a system endure for long?

GRAHAM HUTTON
The Burden of Plenty?, 1935

[413] Whilst . . . the enlargement of the functions of government involved in the task of adjusting to one another the propensity to consume and the inducement to invest, would seem to a nineteenth-century publicist or to a contemporary American financier to be a terrific encroachment on individualism, I defend it, on the contrary, both as the only practicable means of avoiding the destruction of existing economic forms in their entirety and as the condition of the successful functioning of individual initiative.

For if effective demand is deficient, not only is the public scandal of wasted resources intolerable, but the individual enterpriser who seeks to bring these resources into action is operating with the odds loaded against him.

JOHN MAYNARD KEYNES
The General Theory of Employment, Interest and Money, 1936

[414] Ancient Egypt was doubly fortunate, and doubtless owed to this its fabled wealth, in that it possessed *two* activities, namely, pyramid-building as well as the search for the precious metals, the fruits of which, since they could not serve the needs of man by being consumed, did not stale with abundance. The Middle Ages built cathedrals and sang dirges. Two pyramids, two masses for the dead, are twice as good as one; but not so two railways from London to York.

JOHN MAYNARD KEYNES
The General Theory of Employment, Interest and Money, 1936

[415] In a country where the sole employer is the State,

opposition means death by slow starvation. The old principle: who does not work shall not eat, has been replaced by a new one: who does not obey shall not eat.

LEON TROTSKY
1937

[416] The economic prerequisites for the proletarian revolution have already in general achieved the highest point of maturity that can be reached under capitalism. Mankind's productive forces stagnate. Already new inventions and improvements fail to raise the level of material wealth. Cyclical slumps, under the conditions of the social crisis of the whole capitalistic system inflict ever heavier deprivations and sufferings upon the masses. Growing unemployment, in its turn, deepens the financial crisis of the state and undermines the unstable monetary systems. Democratic as well as Fascist régimes stagger on from one bankruptcy to another.

The bourgeoisie itself sees no way out. In countries where it has already been forced to stake its last upon the card of fascism, it now toboggans with closed eyes toward an economic and military catastrophe. LEON TROTSKY
The Death Agony of Capitalism, 1938

[417] People, in choosing their investments . . . place their resources in such a way that, on the average and on the whole, the marginal yield works out about equally in different occupations. In these circumstances it is obvious that any general State policy of cutting down prices in any industry below the competitive level, on occasions when the conditions of demand and supply would enable that industry to obtain exceptional profits, must, in effect, penalize it

as compared with stable industries. For, if, in a hilly district where the average level of peaks and valleys is the same as it is on a plateau, the tops of the peaks are removed, the average level there will, of course, be reduced below that of the plateau.

ARTHUR CECIL PIGOU
Economics of Welfare, 1920

[418] The publication by the Government of a plan covering all aspects of the country's economic development for the next five years is a major advance in economic policy-making in the United Kingdom. Prepared in the fullest consultation with industry, the plan for the first time represents a statement of Government policy and a commitment to action by the Government.

. . . Increasing our output by 25 per cent may seem an ambitious aim at a time when balance of payments considerations limit the short run possibilities for expansion. But in reality the immediate situation makes it essential that industry must plan its investment, manning and training in order to achieve this result. If industry is to do this, it must have a clear picture of the potential growth of the economy four or five years ahead: this the Plan provides.

GEORGE BROWN, M.P.
Foreword to *The National Plan* (Cmnd 2764), 1965

[419] It is, it seems, practically impossible for a capitalist democracy to organize expenditure on the scale necessary to prove my case—except under war conditions.

JOHN MAYNARD KEYNES
New Republic, 20 July, 1940

[420] Careful planning becomes a necessity as soon as you begin to realize that *laissez-faire* is not enough; and it be-

comes necessary on a scale we have hardly begun to envisage once you deliberately throw *laissez-faire* and economic man into the discard, and set about building a truly organized, living community. JULIAN HUXLEY

Democracy Marches, 1941

[421] Social security must be achieved by co-operation between the State and the individual. The State should offer security for service and contribution. The State in organizing security should not stifle incentive, opportunity, responsibility; in establishing a national minimum, it should leave room and encouragement for voluntary action by each individual to provide more than that minimum for himself and his family. SIR WILLIAM BEVERIDGE

Report on Social Insurance and Allied Services, 1942

[422] Karl Marx, as a religious leader, is analogous to both Confucius and Bentham. His ethical doctrine, in a nutshell, is this: that every man pursues the economic interest of his class, and therefore, if there is only one class every man will pursue the general interest. This doctrine has failed to work out in practice as its adherents expected, both because men do not in fact pursue the interest of their class, and because no civilized community is possible in which there is only one class, since government and executive officials are unavoidable. BERTRAND RUSSELL

Freedom and Government, 1942

[423] Communists, who are often regarded as enemies of freedom, lay great stress on the fact that in practice many kinds of freedom, though not legally or customarily restricted, are economically restricted, so that they are

the privileges of a small minority. 'Liberty', they claim, 'is such a precious thing that it must be rationed.'

J. B. S. HALDANE
A Comparative Study of Freedom, 1942

[424] There is nothing wrong with the pure logic of socialism.

J. A. SCHUMPETER
Capitalism, Socialism and Democracy, 1943

[425] The question raised by economic planning is . . . merely whether we shall be able to satisfy what we regard as our more or less important needs in the way we prefer. It is whether it shall be we who decide what is more, and what is less, important for us, or whether this is to be decided by the planner. Economic planning would not affect merely those of our marginal needs that we have in mind when we speak contemptuously about the merely economic. It would, in effect, mean that we as individuals should no longer be allowed to decide what we regard as marginal.

The authority directing all economic activity would control not merely the part of our lives which is concerned with inferior things; it would control the allocation of the limited means for all our ends. And whoever controls all economic activity controls the means for all our ends, and must therefore decide which are to be satisfied and which not. This is really the crux of the matter.

F. A. HAYEK
The Road to Serfdom, 1944

[426] The movement for planning owes its present strength largely to the fact that, while planning is in the main still an ambition, it units almost all the single-minded idealists, all the men and women who have devoted their lives to a single task. The hopes they place in planning, however, are

not the result of a comprehensive view of society, but rather of a very limited view, and often the result of a great exaggeration of the importance of the ends they place foremost. This is not to underrate the great pragmatic value of this type of men in a free society like ours, which makes them the subject of just admiration. But it would make the very men who are most anxious to plan society the most dangerous if they were allowed to do so—and the most intolerant of the planning of others. From the saintly and single-minded idealist to the fanatic is often but a step.

Though it is the resentment of the frustrated specialist which gives the demand for planning its strongest impetus, there could hardly be a more unbearable—and more irrational—world than one in which the most eminent specialists in each field were allowed to proceed unchecked with the realization of their ideals. Nor can 'co-ordination', as some planners seem to imagine, become a new specialism. The economist is the last to claim that he has the knowledge which the co-ordinator would need. His plea is for a method which effects such co-ordination without the need for an omniscient dictator. But that means precisely the retention of some such impersonal and often unintelligible checks on individual efforts as those against which all specialists chafe.

F. A. HAYEK
The Road to Serfdom, 1944

[427] Only an organizing genius could produce a shortage of coal and fish in Great Britain. ANEURIN BEVAN, M.P.
At the Labour Party Conference, 1945

[428] When we went into the economic and financial smash of 1931 we did not know we were going there . . . because

there was no proper machinery of the State to tell us, and when we got there we did not know fully what to do about it. . . . We are determined that we are not going to be caught unawares by blind economic forces under this Administration. HERBERT MORRISON, M.P.

At the Labour Party Conference, 1946

[429] The real contrast between planned and unplanned economies appears to have two aspects. In the mainly planned economy, there is an attempt to regulate total production, in order to ensure full employment and the fullest possible use of the available resources; and there is also an attempt to decide in advance what proportions of manpower and other resources are to be devoted to the main alternative uses—how much to producing capital goods and how much to consumer's goods, and how much to each main sort of each. It is of the essence of a mainly planned economy not to leave either the total amount of production or its nature to be settled by the separate decisions of a large number of independent producers, but to attempt to settle both, on broad lines at least, through public bodies responsible to the Government, and acting under its Authority. As against this, in a mainly planless economy, there is *normally* no attempt to settle either the total volume of production or its distribution among various kinds of goods and services, though there may be 'planning' to increase or decrease the volume of production of certain particular kinds, e.g. more food, more houses, less whisky, or even, under our topsy-turvy economic arrangements fewer ships, less steel or coal, fewer hogs, or less coffee or rubber.

G. D. H. COLE

The Intelligent Man's Guide to the Post-War World, 1947

[430] Marxism is not only a theory of history. It is a way of making history happen.

BARBARA WARD
The West at Bay, 1948

[431] Marxism is only an episode—one of the many mistakes we have made in the perennial and dangerous struggle for building a better and a freer world.

K. R. POPPER
Preface to Revised Edition of *The Open Society and Its Enemies*, 1952

[432] This idea of economic planning has commonly been related to Marx and Marxism. This is a factual mistake. I do not believe that the term 'economic planning' or 'planned economy' can be found in Marx's work. Marx was not a planner but an analyst and a forecaster.

GUNNAR MYRDAL
Beyond the Welfare State, 1960

[433] The British have formed the habit of praising their institutions, which are sometimes inept, and of ignoring the character of their race, which is often superb. In the end they will be in danger of losing their character and being left with their institutions: a result disastrous indeed.

LORD RADCLIFFE
The Problem of Power, 1952

[434] The individual citizen is lost in a jungle of benefits, doles, subsidies and pensions from which he can do no other than grab what he can; and of rules, restraints and charges from which he strives to escape. He is no longer governed by the natural laws of political economy but is reduced to scheming to secure from the common pool more than he puts into it.

SIR ERNEST BENN
The State the Enemy, 1953

[435] Let's find out what everyone is doing
And then stop everyone from doing it.

A. P. HERBERT
'Let's Stop Somebody' (song in revue), 1930

[436] The doctrine of the safety net, to catch those who fall, has been made meaningless by the doctrine of fair shares for those of us who are quite able to stand.

The Economist, 15 March, 1958

[437] There is a limit to the Welfare State, and that limit is the capacity of the British nation to pay for it. . . . If the choice has to be made between a new factory making machine tools in Coventry or a new hospital in my constituency of Pembrokeshire, I should unhesitatingly decide on the machine tool factory, because that is how we would get the better hospital in the end.

DESMOND DONNELLY, M.P.
Speech to the Labour Party Conference, October 1958

[438] Given the present and prospective state of knowledge about economic relationships, the labour required for economic calculation, and the fact that the most important decision problems are unique experiments, it is inevitable that economic policy-makers and commentators must rely to a large extent on guessing at the magnitudes of economic effects. What is objectionable is guesswork which produces a final conclusion without either reducing the area within which guesswork is necessary as far as possible, or defining as clearly as possible the nature of the guess and the factors considered in making it. Such guesswork has the undesirable effect of implying that one man's guess is as good as another's,

and that there is no great need to try to reduce the area of ignorance.

HARRY G. JOHNSON
The Free Trade Proposals, 1960

[439] It is the character rather than the volume of government activity that is important. A functioning market economy presupposes certain activities on the part of the State; there are some other such activities by which its functioning will be assisted; and it can tolerate many more, provided that they are of the kind which are compatible with a functioning market. But there are those which run counter to the very principle on which a free system rests and which must therefore be altogether excluded if such a system is to work. In consequence, a government that is comparatively inactive but does the wrong things may do much more to cripple the forces of a market economy than one that is more concerned with economic affairs but confines itself to actions which assist the spontaneous forces of that economy.

F. A. HAYEK
The Constitution of Liberty, 1960

[440] Marx expected that a socialist revolution would have only to expropriate the expropriators, to take over a highly developed industrial economy as a going concern. As it turns out, socialist economies have to carry out industrialization for themselves, and they have to contend with feudal property relations and ancient ideologies which capitalism failed to break down. The orthodox economist, who cannot approve of socialism or of feudalism either, finds himself sadly bewildered.

JOAN ROBINSON
Economic Philosophy, 1962

[441] The concentration of economic power that Marx foresaw has come to pass. The main structure of latter-day capitalism consists in a few large enterprises dominating each industry with a fringe of small business growing and declining around them. The enterprise takes on a kind of organic life of its own and commands the loyalty of successive generations of executives. But Marx's prediction that capitalism would grow correspondingly fiercer has not proved correct. The motives that impel the modern enterprise cannot really be described as merely the pursuit of profit. Certainly profits are its object and its mark of success but it needs profits in order to grow, rather than wanting to grow in order to make more profits. As productivity increases, part of the benefit is passed on to keep the workers quiet, for industrial strife is not helpful to growth. The managers know very well that if each invests all will flourish; they are by no means averse to a Government policy 'favourable to faster growth' even if it means that they have to accept some limitations on their freedom in order to fit in with a general scheme. . . . *Laissez-faire* ideology is no longer appropriate. JOAN ROBINSON

'The Final End of Laissez-Faire', *Collected Economic Papers*, 1965

[442] State planning suffers from the psychological disadvantage that the achievement drives of the people who are doing the everyday work are frustrated and consequently their performance is often below their potential. This damage has become widely recognized even in Russia and Eastern Europe where, although planning is an ideological commitment, they are now tumbling over one another to escape its meshes. The communist experience is further

evidence that psychological satisfaction and economic efficiency lie in the freedom of the market economy.

RICHARD LYNN
National Planning and Industrial Frustration, 1967

[443] Planners have an inevitable prejudice against anything liable to upset their predictions. Competition, for example can play hell with the best laid plans; planners therefore have, a penchant for monopoly. Foreign trade can be particularly intractable; hence a preference among planners for autarchy. . . . Public consumption tends to be given priority over private consumption because the former is more amenable to control. Private consumption is liable to break out in unexpected directions and though in theory it can be restricted by fiscal means, private consumers have an awkward habit of insisting on maintaining their standard of living by means of wage rises.

Again, there is the prejudice very rife among economists, and among planners in particular, in favour of the measurable. Given that economic growth is invariably at least one of the ends of planning, planners tend to value those human activities (essentially transactions) which contribute to GDP to the detriment of those which do not because no monetary value can be placed on them. Similarly, in analysing the factors conducive to growth planners tend to take more seriously those which are susceptible of measurement, the prize example being investment. Those which defy conventional statistical yardsticks—confidence factors, managerial quality, entrepreneurial flair—are discounted consciously or unconsciously.

Most serious of all perhaps is the impatience which many planners seem to feel with politics. Although they may admit that the objectives of the Plan are politically determined, they are naturally loath to accept the right of politicians to tamper with their Plan once it is under way. But the implications of this attitude are deeply undemocratic, threatening the whole supremacy of the legislature.

Any claim that the planners may make to objectivity is therefore spurious.

JOHN BRUNNER
The Plan that Failed, 1967

[444] I am inclined to believe it was a mistake of some Marxian economists, who had great influence on the formation of the traditional socialist economic system, to suppose that macro-economic laws could be enforced only in a battle against micro-economic laws. That is how a socialist economy retained the concepts of the market system but did not make use of market laws. On the contrary, it fought against them. For half a century this hypothesis was attacked again and again by some socialist economists, but only in the past decade has it been generally recognised that plan and market are not antagonistic. Planned development and economic efficiency can be ensured by the existence of market regulations. Socialist economies are pursuing this method but, of course, with some differences in individual countries.

BELA CSIKOS-NAGY
Pricing in Hungary, 1968

[445] In any attempt . . . by planning bodies still retaining their sovereignty, to fit together their national plans, the world economy is doomed from the outset. For the plans will not fit and the attempts to make them fit will degenerate quickly into cynical and unscrupulous bargaining in which the only men not allowed to speak at the conference

—the ordinary customer and the free producer and merchant—will be squeezed flat against the wall. Each planned economy will be trying to do the same thing; to increase exports and reduce imports; to invest heavily in capital equipment and in the basic industries, and, for this purpose, to borrow from the others; to build up uneconomic industries so that it can bargain more effectively at the table of the international conference. The prolonged negotiations will always be outstripped by the economic facts of the time. So the conferences will break up in confusion with binding agreements, always subject to waiver, phrased in grandiloquent but meaningless terms, and with arrangements to set up futile 'study groups' which can only waste more time. And so the delegates will go home, wearied with their life on the treadmill, convinced of the unreasonableness of the foreigner, and more than ever certain that in the international babel their country must stand on its own feet, which means in effect that it must also stand on the economic jugular vein of some other country.

JOHN JEWKES
The New Ordeal by Planning, 1968

[446] We were socialists because Individualism for us meant muddle, meant a crowd of separated, undisciplined little people all obstinately and ignorantly doing things jarringly, each in his own way. . . . Order and devotion were the very essence of our discipline and a splendid collective vigour and happiness its end. We projected an ideal state, an organized state as confident and powerful as modern science, the organized state that should end muddle for ever. . . .

H. G. WELLS
The New Machiavelli, 1911

[447] We have begun to grope our way towards a practical concept of economic planning which may prove in a few years time, to be as revolutionary in its implications as was the Keynesian revolution in economics thirty years ago.

New Frontiers for Social Policy, Labour Party policy document, 1963

[448] What optimists we were! We had only to eradicate the profit system, to replace private with public ownership, and all problems would be at an end. Not only would booms and slumps, disappear and work become available for everyone but the whole climate of society would be transformed.

Since workers would own the fields and factories, there would be no more strikes. Since co-operation would replace competition, personal relationships would improve. Since no one would any longer need to steal to keep his children properly fed, crime would rapidly diminish. Since great literature, music and art would become accessible to all, all would become lovers of Shakespeare, Beethoven and Van Gogh. Filled with a glowing consciousness of common purpose, the lives of all of us would have meaning and significance.

Yes, we were wrong; but let no one say we were wrong in a mean or selfish manner.

CHRISTOPHER MAYHEW, M.P.
Party Games, 1969

VIII

A Free Economy

[449] All men seek one goal: success or happiness. The only way to achieve true success is to express yourself completely in service to society. First, have a definite, clear, practical ideal—a goal, an objective. Second, have the necessary means to achieve your ends—wisdom, money, materials, and methods. Third, adjust your means to that end.

ARISTOTLE
c. 340 B.C. Quoted in *Harvard Business Review*, Jan./Feb. 1968

[450] All free subjects are born inheritable, as to their land, and also as to the free exercise of their industry, in those trades whereto they apply themselves and whereby they live.
A Committee of the House of Commons, 1604

[451] Away from the cant of 'measures, not men'!—the idle supposition that it is the harness and not the horses that draw the chariot along.
GEORGE CANNING
1770–1827

[452] The more perfect civilization is, the less occasion has it for Government.
THOMAS PAINE
The Rights of Man, 1792

[453] My opinion is against an overdoing of any sort of administration, and more especially against this most momentous of all meddling on the part of authority: the meddling with the subsistence of the people.

EDMUND BURKE
Thoughts and Details upon Scarcity, 1795

[454] I am not aware that any community has a right to force another to be civilized.
JOHN STUART MILL
On Liberty, 1859

[455] Distrust in government is healthy; in Britain the performance even of governments that in principle have believed in limited government does not inspire confidence that they are sufficiently free from the pressures of interest or expediency to serve the common good. But organized society must run the risk of bad or indifferent government. The question is 'Which kind?'. For many years in Britain and elsewhere economists and other social scientists have tried to design institutions for centralized economic direction by the State and its organs. In time they may perhaps evolve arrangements that avoid the defects displayed in their constructions so far. But if we are to make an informed choice between the two systems of society there is also need for economists to keep up to date and refine their study of the institutions of a market economy. ARTHUR SELDON

Agenda for a Free Society, 1961

[456] Above this race of men stands an immense and tutelary power, which takes upon itself alone to secure their gratifications and to watch over their fate. That power is absolute, minute, regular, provident and mild. It would be like the authority of a parent if, like that authority, its object was to prepare men for manhood; but it seeks, on the contrary, to keep them in perpetual childhood. It is well content that the people should rejoice, provided they think of nothing but rejoicing. For their happiness such a government willingly labours, but it chooses to be the sole agent and the only arbiter of that happiness. It provides for their security, foresees and supplies their necessities, facilitates their pleasures, directs their industry, regulates the descent of property and subdivides their inheritances—what re-

mains but to spare them all the care of thinking and all the trouble of living?

The will of man is not shattered, but softened, bent and guided; men are seldom forced by it to act, but they are constantly restrained from acting. Such a power does not destroy but it prevents existence. It does not tyrannize, but it compresses, enervates, extinguishes and stupifies a people, until each nation is reduced to be nothing better than a flock of timid and industrious animals, of which the government is the shepherd. ALEXIS DE TOCQUEVILLE

Democracy in America, 1835

[457] As practical beings it is our business to free human life from as many as possible of its difficulties, and not to keep up a stock of them as hunters preserve game, for the exercise of pursuing it. JOHN STUART MILL

Principles of Political Economy, 1848

[458] It is a common error of the people who are called wise and practical in ordinary times, to judge by certain rules the men whose very object is to change or to destroy those rules. When a time is come at which passion takes the guidance of affairs, the beliefs of men of experience are less worthy of consideration than the schemes which engage the imagination of dreamers. ALEXIS DE TOCQUEVILLE

On the State of Society in France before the Revolution of 1789. Trans. 1873

[459] When the State ceaseth, look, my brothers—do you not see the rainbows and the bridges of the Beyond?

F. W. NIETZSCHE

Thus Spake Zarathustra, 1896

[460] Human happiness, according to the most received

notions, seems to consist of three ingredients: action, pleasure, and indolence. And though these ingredients ought to be mixed in different proportions, according to the particular disposition of the person, yet no one ingredient can be entirely wanting, without destroying, in some measure, the relish of the whole composition. Indolence, or repose, indeed, seems not of itself to contribute much to our enjoyment; but, like sleep, is requisite as an indulgence to the weakness of human nature, which cannot support an uninterrupted course of business or pleasure. That quick march of the spirits, which takes a man from himself, and chiefly gives satisfaction, does in the end exhaust the mind, and requires some intervals of repose, which, though agreeable for a moment, yet, if prolonged, beget a languor and lethargy that destroys all enjoyment. Education, custom, and example, have a mighty influence in turning the mind to any of these pursuits; and it must be owned, that, where they promote a relish for action and pleasure, they are so favourable to human happiness. In times when industry and the arts flourish, men are kept in perpetual occupation, and enjoy, as their reward, the occupation itself, as well as those pleasures which are the fruits of their labour. The mind acquires new vigour; enlarges its powers and faculties; and by an assiduity in honest industry, both satisfies its natural appetites, and prevents the growth of unnatural ones, which commonly spring up, when nourished by ease and idleness. Banish those arts from society, you deprive men both of action and pleasure. . . . DAVID HUME

Of Refinement in the Arts, 1752

[461] The man of system . . . is apt to be very wise in his own conceit; and is often so enamoured with the supposed

beauty of his own ideal plan of government, that he cannot suffer the smallest deviation from any part of it. . . . He seems to imagine that he can arrange the different members of a great society with as much ease as the hand that arranges the different pieces upon a chessboard. He does not consider that the pieces upon the chessboard have no other principle of motion besides that which the hand impresses on them; but that, in the great chessboard of human society, every single piece has a principle of motion of its own, altogether different from that which the legislature might choose to impress upon it. If those two principles coincide and act in the same direction, the game of human society will go on easily and harmoniously, and is very likely to be happy and successful. If they are opposite or different, the game will go on miserably, and the society must be at all times in the highest degree of disorder.

ADAM SMITH
The Theory of Moral Sentiments, 1759

[462] The progressive state is in reality the cheerful and the hearty state to all the different orders of society. The stationary is dull; the declining, melancholy.

ADAM SMITH
The Wealth of Nations, 1775

[463] With the view of causing an increase to take place in the mass of national wealth, or with a view to increase the means either of subsistence or enjoyment, without some special reason, the general rule is, that nothing ought to be done or attempted by government. The motto, or watchword, of government on these occasions ought to be—*Be quiet*. . . . The request which agriculture, manufacturers, and

commerce present to governments is modest and reasonable as that which Diogenes made to Alexander: '*Stand out of my sunshine*'. We have no need of favour—we require only a secure and open path. JEREMY BENTHAM
Manual of Political Economy, 1798

[464] The abolition of private ownership of the means of production would constitute the abolition of the institution of property itself, and that in turn would involve the destruction of all forms of freedom. It would wipe out the one-man show and with it the solid core of independence and non-conformity which has traditionally been bred in such surroundings, not to mention the steady flow of enterprise and variety which it has infused into the economic system. It would wipe out the merchant. It would impose cramping restrictions on those who are temperamentally attracted by the task of taking risks, organizing or innovating. It would restrict all choice of occupation except that approved by the State. It would deprive people of the right to save except under such conditions which make them more completely subservient to the State. And, by preventing the creation of a class with a measure of financial independence, it would enfeeble the expression of unpopular minority views which represent the salt and savour of any society and so often constitute, in one generation, what comes to be accepted as the wisdom of the following.

JOHN JEWKES
The New Ordeal by Planning, 1968

[465] How are you to do without a government? And what other government, if this Bill be ultimately lost, could possibly be found? How could any country defray the

ruinous expense of protecting, with troops and constables, the Duke of Wellington and Sir Robert Peel, who literally would not be able to walk from the Horse Guards to Grosvenor Square without two or three regiments of foot to screen them from the mob; and in these hollow squares the Hero of Waterloo would have to spend his political life. . . .

The majority of the new members will be landed gentlemen: their genus is utterly distinct from the revolutionary tribe; they have Molar teeth; they are destitute of the carnivorous and incisive jaws of political adventurers.

There will be mistakes at first, as there are in all changes. All young ladies will imagine (as soon as this Bill is carried) that they will instantly be married; Schoolboys believe that Gerunds and Supines will be abolished, and that Currant Tarts must ultimately come down in price; the Corporal and Sergeant are sure of double pay; bad Poets will expect a demand for their Epics; Fools will be disappointed, as they always are; reasonable men, who know what to expect, will find that a very serious good has been obtained. . . .

Reform will produce economy and investigation; there will be fewer jobs, and a less lavish expenditure; wars will not be persevered in for years after the people are tired of them; taxes will be taken off the poor and laid upon the rich; demotic habits will be more common in a country where the rich are forced to court the poor for popularity. . . .

We do not pretend to abolish poverty, or to prevent wretchedness; but if peace, economy, and justice are the results of Reform, a number of small benefits—or rather of benefits which appear small to us—will accrue to millions of the people.

REV. SYDNEY SMITH
Speech on the Reform Bill, 1831

[466] I think that democratic communities have a natural taste for freedom; left to themselves, they will seek it, cherish it, and view any privation of it with regret. But for equality, their passion is ardent, insatiable, incessant, invincible: they call for equality in freedom; and if they cannot obtain that, they will still call for equality in slavery.

ALEXIS DE TOCQUEVILLE
Democracy in America, 1835

[467] An acre in Middlesex is better than a principality in Utopia.

LORD MACAULAY
On Lord Bacon, *Essays*, 1843

[468] God has given to men all that is necessary for them to accomplish their destinies. He has provided a social form as well as a human form. And these social organs of persons are so constituted that they will develop themselves harmoniously as in the clean air of liberty. Away, then, with quacks and organizers! Away with their rings, chains, hooks, and pincers! Away with their artificial systems! Away with the whims of governmental administrators, their socialized projects, their centralization, their tariffs, their government schools, their state religions, their free credit, their bank monopolies, their regulations, their restrictions, their equalization by taxation, and their pious moralizations!

And now that the legislators and do-gooders have so futilely inflicted so many systems upon society, may they finally end where they should have begun: May they reject all systems, and try liberty; for liberty is an acknowledgment of faith in God and His works.

FREDERIC BASTIAT
The Law, 1850

[469] Man cannot direct his efforts to the satisfaction of

moral wants of the highest and most elevated kind until after he has provided for those which concern his preservation and sustenance. Whence, without going further, we may conclude that every legislative measure which tells against the material well-being of communities injures the moral life of nations.

FREDERIC BASTIAT
Harmonies of Political Economy, 1860

[470] Under the Government of Sir Robert Peel, in 1846, the law was repealed, and three years afterwards—in 1849—all the duties on these articles were taken off, except a shilling per quarter, which has been more recently abolished. Since this happened there has been no fall of rents throughout the kingdom. In point of fact the prosperity of the country has been so increased that the rent of land throughout the country is now higher than it was when that Corn Law was in existence, and the farmers, who were always complaining, during the existence of that law, have scarcely ever been heard to complain in the least since it was abolished.

They complained for a year or two because they had been greatly frightened, but there has never been, I will say, within the last hundred years a period when the farmers of this country have made less complaint to the public or to Parliament than they have during the last thirty years since the law for their protection was abolished. And what happened to the labourer? The wages of farm-labourers have risen on the whole much more, I believe, than 50 per cent. throughout the whole country; and in some counties and districts, I believe, the farm labourer at this moment is receiving double the wages he was when this law was in existence.

We ought to learn from this what a grand thing it is to

establish our laws upon a basis of freedom and justice. It blesses him who gives and him who takes. It has blessed all our manufacturing districts with a steadiness of employment and an abundance they never knew before, and it has blessed not less the very class who in their dark terror and blindness thought that they could have profited by that which was so unjust, so cruel to the bulk of their countrymen.

JOHN BRIGHT
In a speech at Rochdale on 2 January, 1877

[471] The doctrine of self-reliance and self-denial, which is the foundation of political economy, was written as legibly in *The New Testament* as in *The Wealth of Nations.*

LORD ACTON
1907

[472] Either everything in man can be traced as a development from below, or something must come from above. There is no avoiding that dilemma: you must either be a naturalist or a supernaturalist. If you remove from the word 'human' all that the belief in the supernatural has given to man, you can view him finally as no more than an extremely clever, adaptable and mischievous little animal.

T. S. ELIOT
Second Thoughts about Humanism, 1929

[473] The literary exposition of freedom deals mainly with the frills. The Greek myth was more to the point. Prometheus did not bring to mankind freedom of the press. He procured fire, which obediently to human purpose cooks and gives warmth. In fact, freedom of action is a primary human need. In modern thought, the expression of this

truth has taken the form of 'the economic interpretation of history'.

ALFRED NORTH WHITEHEAD
Adventures of Ideas, 1933

[474] The fact is that these ancient philosophers were not and could not be economists in our sense of persons who are interested in and think and perhaps talk or write about the material welfare of mankind. They professed to be concerned with higher things, and if they were not always so in fact, it was because they thought of themselves rather than because they thought of their fellow men. Their State, of which they made so much, covered a contemptible little district with one small town in it and a population of which the great majority were not citizens but slaves. It was impossible for economics to develop in such an environment.

EDWIN CANNAN
A Review of Economic Theory, 1929

[475] No particular man is necessary to the state. We may depend on it that, if we provide the country with popular institutions, those institutions will provide it with great men.

LORD MACAULAY
1800–1859

[476] The advantage to efficiency of the decentralization of decisions and of individual responsibility is even greater, perhaps, than the nineteenth century supposed; and the reaction against the appeal to self-interest may have gone too far. But, above all, Individualism if it can be purged of its defects and its abuses, is the best safeguard of personal liberty in the sense that it greatly widens the field for the exercise of personal choice. It is also the best safeguard of

the variety of life, which emerges precisely from this extended field of personal choice, and the loss of which is the greatest of all losses of the homogeneous or totalitarian state. For this variety preserves the traditions which embody the most secure and successful choices of former generations; it colours the present with the diversification of its fancy; and, being the handmaiden of experiment as well as of tradition and of fancy, it is the most powerful instrument to better the future. JOHN MAYNARD KEYNES

The General Theory of Employment, Interest and Money, 1936

[477] A human being feels an obligation only if he is free, and each obligation, considered separately, implies liberty. But it is necessary that there should be obligations; and the deeper we go, away from those particular obligations which are at the top, towards obligation in general . . . which is at the bottom, the more obligation appears as the very form assumed by necessity in the realm of life, when it demands for the accomplishment of certain ends intelligence, choice and therefore liberty. HENRI BERGSON

The Two Sources of Morality and Religion, 1942

[478] Make the strongest case you can against democratic government and it yet remains the only political system in which men are recognized to possess an equal claim upon the common stock of welfare. Alternative systems, however admirably they may begin, always end by protecting the interests of the few. HAROLD J. LASKI

Nationalism and the Future of Civilization, 1942

[479] Every man desires freedom for his own impulses, but men's impulses conflict, and therefore not all can be satisfied. In the first place, we desire more than our fair share of

possessions; this can be met, in theory, by decreeing equality of distribution, as has been done by the institution of monogamy. But there is a more essential and deep-rooted conflict owing to the love of power: most human beings, though in varying degrees, desire to control, not only their own lives but also the lives of others.

BERTRAND RUSSELL
Freedom and Government, 1942

[480] Cromwell spent the first half of his career in agitation connected with draining the Fens, and the second in making himself a military dictator. In other circumstances, his power impulses might have found only the earlier beneficent outlet. If freedom is to be secure, it is essential both that useful careers shall be open to energetic men, and the harmful careers shall be closed to them.

BERTRAND RUSSELL
Freedom and Government, 1942

[481] Democracy itself was once a revolution. Today it is the greatest conservative power upon earth.

THOMAS MANN
Freedom and Equality, 1942

[482] Our intellectual as well as our ethical education is corrupt. It is perverted by the admiration of brilliance, of the way things are said, which takes the place of a critical appreciation of the things that are said (and the things that are done). It is perverted by the romantic idea of the splendour of the stage of History on which we are the actors. We are educated to act with an eye to the gallery.

K. R. POPPER
The Open Society and Its Enemies, 1945

[483] Society has always to demand a little more from human beings than it will get in practice. . . . I never read the proclamations of generals before battles, the speeches of fuhrers and prime ministers, the solidarity songs of public schools and Left Wing political parties, national anthems, Temperance tracts, papal encyclicals and sermons against gambling and contraception, without seeming to hear in the background a chorus of raspberries from all the millions of common men to whom these high sentiments make no appeal. Nevertheless the high sentiments always win in the end, leaders who offer blood, toil, tears and sweat always get more out of their followers than those who offer safety and a good time. When it comes to the pinch, human beings are heroic.

GEORGE ORWELL
'The Art of Donald McGill', *Critical Essays*, 1946

[484] It isn't as if we had had any choice. What we had to do in this situation was to loosen the shackles. We had to be prepared to restore basic moral principles and to start with a purge of the economy of our society.

We have done more, by turning from a State-controlled economy to a market economy, than merely introduce economic measures. We have laid new foundations for our social and economic life. We had to abjure all intolerance which, from a spiritual lack of freedom, leads to tyranny and totalitarianism. We had to strive for an order which by voluntary regrouping and a sense of responsibility would lead to a sensible organic whole.

LUDWIG ERHARD
Speech in the British Zone of Occupied Germany, 1948

[485] The State is or can be master of money, but in a free society it is master of very little else. The making of a

good society depends not on the State but on the citizens, acting individually or in free association with one another, acting on motives of various kinds, some selfish others unselfish, some narrow and material others inspired by love of man and love of God. The happiness or unhappiness of the society in which we live depends upon ourselves as citizens, not on the instrument of political power which we call the State.
LORD BEVERIDGE
Voluntary Action: a Report on Methods of Social Advance, 1948

[486] When the facts of international economic inequalities and their tendency to grow are confronted with the state of public conscience in the richer nations and with the economic theory which has developed in the cultural setting of those countries, discords are brought into the open both in the moral and the intellectual spheres.

Of these the moral discord is undoubtedly the fundamental one. On the one hand, there is in these nations, a the general plane of valuations, a common adherence to the ideal, inherited from far back in history, of the right of all persons to equality of opportunity, irrespective of race and colour, religion and creed, social status and nationality. On the other hand, in their daily life as individuals and as citizens, people there are not, in fact, prepared to take the consequences of this great moral principle, in a measure which even remotely approached completeness.

Economic theory is only a segment of the total culture. It becomes modulated to serve opportunistic rationalization needs. In order to live on as comfortably as possible with the moral discord in their hearts, people there need an economic theory that diverts attention from this moral discord.
GUNNAR MYRDAL
Economic Theory and Under-developed Regions, 1957

[487] Letting a hundred flowers blossom and a hundred schools of thought contend is the policy for promoting the progress of the arts and the sciences and a flourishing socialist culture in our land. Different forms and styles in art should develop freely and different schools in science should contend freely. We think that it is harmful to the growth of art and science if administrative measures are used to impose one particular style of art or school of thought and to ban another. Questions of right and wrong in the arts and sciences should be settled through free discussion in artistic and scientific fields. They should not be settled in summary fashion.

MAO TSE-TUNG
27 February, 1957. From the *Quotations*

[488] If we wish to deal with economic and historical forces, we must begin by rejecting the fatalism we have absorbed from Marxist philosophy. We must accept the fact that crises and recessions, like prosperity, are man-made and that, to a large extent, they are the reflection of a people's psychology and of its outlook on life. There is nothing mysterious and there is nothing inevitable about the future. It is ours to mould.

ERNEST DICHTER
The Strategy of Desire, 1960

[489] The importance of freedom . . . does not depend on the elevated character of the activities it makes possible. Freedom of action, even in humble things, is as important as freedom of thought. It has become a common practice to disparage freedom of action by calling it 'economic liberty'. But the concept of freedom of action is much wider than that of economic liberty, which it includes, and, what is more important, it is very questionable whether there are any

actions which can be called merely 'economic' and whether any restrictions on liberty can be confined to what are called merely 'economic' aspects. Economic considerations are merely those by which we reconcile and adjust our different purposes, none of which, in the last resort, are economic. . . .

F. A. HAYEK
The Constitution of Liberty, 1960

[490] The human story does not always unfold like a mathematical calculation on the principle that two and two make four. Sometimes in life they make five or minus three; and sometimes the blackboard topples down in the middle of the sum and leaves the class in disorder and the pedagogue with a black eye.

WINSTON CHURCHILL
1874–1965

[491] It would be a waste of time to spend further powder and shot on the conceptions of pure *laissez-faire*. Indeed, at this time of day, it would perhaps be more appropriate not so much to point out where it was wrong but rather to draw attention to the respects in which it was magnificently right—for at least its advocates were believers in freedom, at least they understood the working of the market, at least they saw through the sophistries of some paternalistic systems. But I think it is worth while to have focused thus briefly the deficiencies of their outlook if only to show by way of contrast wherein I suppose the better one to consist. I hope what I have said in this connection will at least assure you that in my conception the system of economic freedom, as Marshall called it, is not a closed system laid up in heaven, so to speak, deducible from a few simple concepts and capable of being transcribed on a couple of

tablets of stone, but an evolving system, part natural growth, part artefact, continually adapting itself or being adapted to new conditions and new knowledge, whose only main general criterion is that it tends towards freedom rather than away from it. LORD ROBBINS

'Freedom and Order', *Politics and Economics*, 1961

[492] No such thing as absolute equality of treatment for all adult citizens, male and female, in economic and political matters has ever been established in any known and natural human society. . . . Against so vast and universal a backcloth for human society, the pretensions of a few intellectuals in the last century or two—monumentally out of touch with the real desires of the overwhelming masses of their fellows—seem overweening. If it had not been for the limited successes of a few Christian closed communities so organized in earlier ages and poorer times, it is to be doubted whether the intellectuals advocating equality of material circumstances for all adult citizens would ever have gained as much support as they did. Once again, what has happened in our century has been aberration. In any case the trend is now the other way, and the coherence of our societies will be the greater for it. GRAHAM HUTTON

'The Individual and Society', *Agenda for a Free Society*, 1961

[493] Economic arrangements play a dual role in the promotion of a free society. On the one hand, freedom in economic arrangements is itself a component of freedom broadly understood, so economic freedom is an end in itself. In the second place, economic freedom is also an indispensable means toward the achievement of political freedom.

The first of these roles of economic freedom needs special emphasis because intellectuals in particular have a strong bias against regarding this aspect of freedom as important. They tend to express contempt for what they regard as material aspects of life, and to regard their own pursuit of allegedly higher values as on a different plane of significance and as deserving of special attention. For most citizens of the country, however, if not for the intellectual, the direct importance of economic freedom is at least comparable in significance to the indirect importance of economic freedom as a means to political freedom.

The citizen of Great Britain, who after World War II was not permitted to spend his vacation in the United States because of exchange control, was being deprived of an essential freedom no less than the citizen of the United States, who was denied the opportunity to spend his vacation in Russia because of his political views. The one was ostensibly an economic limitation on freedom and the other a political limitation, yet there is no essential difference between the two.

MILTON FRIEDMAN
Capitalism and Freedom, 1962

[494] Government can never duplicate the variety and diversity of individual action. At any moment in time, by imposing uniform standards in housing, or nutrition, or clothing, government could undoubtedly improve the level of living of many individuals; by imposing uniform standards in schooling, road construction, or sanitation, central government could undoubtedly improve the level of performance in many local areas and perhaps even on the average of all communities. But in the process, government would replace progress by stagnation, it would substitute

uniform mediocrity for the variety essential for that experimentation which can bring tomorrow's laggards above today's mean.

MILTON FRIEDMAN
Capitalism and Freedom, 1962

[495] Viewed as a means to the end of political freedom, economic arrangements are important because of their effect on the concentration or dispersion of power. The kind of economic organization that provides economic freedom directly, namely, competitive capitalism, also promotes political freedom because it separates economic power from political power and in this way enables the one to offset the other.

Historical evidence speaks with a single voice on the relation between political freedom and a free market. I know of no example in time or place of a society that has been marked by a large measure of political freedom, and that has not also used something comparable to a free market to organize the bulk of economic activity.

MILTON FRIEDMAN
Capitalism and Freedom, 1962

[496] Certainly one must admit that capitalism with full employment which we have known since the war, is an impressive sight—the rapid growth in many countries, the spread of luxury and the reduction of misery; the greater freedom and self-respect of individuals, no longer cringing to keep a job or rotting without one. Corruption, crime and swindling have grown too, but even swindling is more lusty and cheerful in a seller's market.

JOAN ROBINSON
'Beyond Full Employment', *Collected Economic Papers*, 1965

[497] A distaste for difference can drain life out of any society. Such distaste is a popular fad at the moment and, ultimately, it is a threat to freedom. The rage for togetherness and conformism, which extends from the clothes worn by the young to adult attacks on religion as a divisive force, and from a uniformity in schooling to a feeling that both sides of industry should lie down as lion and lamb together, is a growing danger to the free society.

The dislike of difference, of argument, of conflict, the wish for a quiet life at all costs with as little as possible to excite envy or ambition—almost a wish to get back to the peace of the womb—all this is an invitation to governments to extend their power. The right to differ from the majority, and to be protected in that difference by the law, is one of the chief marks of British liberty. But it is a right that rusts in disuse, and if people come to hate difference it is unlikely that difference will be protected.

The Times Educational Supplement, 1966

[498] We must never offer private monopoly as an alternative to public monopoly. We cannot defend the virtues of a competition which we have quietly abolished by trade agreements or merger. Against the threat of nationalization the giant monopolistic combine is defenceless. It is useless to dwell on the dangers of bureaucracy when you are already part of a bureaucracy. By the time the railways had been allowed to abolish competition among themselves—or from the canals—they were obviously ripe for nationalization. And any industry that presents the same sort of target is simply asking for the same sort of fate. It is arguable, it may even be true, that nationalization in such a case may be

harmful. But the public may be hard to convince that this change will even make much difference.

C. NORTHCOTE PARKINSON
'State Monopoly', in *The Case for Capitalism*, 1967

[499] Can we really rely on the 'coarse thumb and finger' of the bureaucrat to mould the good society? It is to the free and multifarious movements of human activity that civilization owes its most notable achievements. If no economic basis were to be left for the enterprise of individuals and small groups, the outlook would be bleak, for we cannot trust the state to supply the need. But we should be faint-hearted if we held that the battle was lost.

G. C. ALLEN
Economic Fact and Fantasy, 1967

[500] When it shall be said in any country in the world, My poor are happy; neither ignorance nor distress is to be found among them; my jails are empty of prisoners, my streets of beggars; the aged are not in want; the taxes are not oppressive; the rational world is my friend, because I am the friend of happiness: When these things can be said, then may that country boast its Constitution and its Government.

THOMAS PAINE
The Rights of Man, 1792

Acknowledgements

C

Acknowledgements

For permission to reproduce copyright material the publishers are indebted to the following:

George Allen & Unwin Ltd, publishers of *The World's Economic Crisis*, for extracts from contributions by Sir Josiah Stamp, Lord Beveridge and J. M. Keynes; *Voluntary Action* by Lord Beveridge; *The Burden of Plenty?* edited by Graham Hutton; *Capitalism, Socialism and Democracy* by J. A. Schumpeter; *The Method of Freedom* by Walter Lippman; *Freedom: Its Meaning*, for extracts from contributions by Harold Laski, Thomas Mann and Bertrand Russell; *The West at Bay* by Barbara Ward; *The History of Western Philosophy* by Bertrand Russell.

G. Bell & Sons Ltd, publishers of *The Acquisitive Society* by R. H. Tawney.

Ernest Benn Ltd, publishers of *The State the Enemy* by Sir Ernest Benn.

Butterworths, publishers of *Introduction to Economics* by Alec Cairncross.

Cambridge University Press, publishers of *Socialism, Capitalism and Economic Growth* (Feinstein) and of *The Years of High Theory* by G. L. S. Shackle.

The Catholic Institute for International Relations, publishers of *Poverty and Politics* by Barbara Ward.

Chatto & Windus Ltd, publishers of *On British Freedom* by Clive Bell; *Democracy Marches* by Julian Huxley; and *Crome Yellow* by Aldous Huxley.

The Clarendon Press, Oxford, publishers of *Value and Capital* by Sir John Hicks.

Darton, Longman and Todd Ltd, publishers of *Britain 1984* by Ronald Brech.

J. M. Dent & Sons Ltd, publishers of *Everyman's Dictionary of Economics*.

Gerald Duckworth & Co Ltd, publishers of *Economic Theory and Under-developed Regions* by Gunnar Myrdal.

The *Economic Journal*, for extracts from contributions by J. M. Keynes.

Encounter, for extracts from contributions by Arthur Koestler and Michael Postan.

Acknowledgements

Rupert Hart-Davis Ltd, publishers of *The End of Laissez-Faire* and *Essays in Persuasion* by J. M. Keynes.

Harvard Business Review and Professor Theodore H. Levitt for extracts from 'Marketing Myopia'.

A. M. Heath & Company Ltd and Miss Sonia Brownell for extracts from *Down and Out in Paris and London* and *Critical Essays* by George Orwell, published by Martin Secker & Warburg Ltd.

Henry Holt & Co., New York, publishers of *Morality and Religion* by Henri Bergson.

Holt, Rinehart and Winston Inc., New York, publishers of *The Two Sources of Morality and Religion* by Henri Bergson; translated by R. Ashley Andra and Cloudesley Brereton with the assistance of W. Horsfall Carter.

The Home University Library, publishers of *Political Economy* by Sir Sydney Chapman.

Houghton Mifflin Company, Boston, U.S.A., publishers of *The Affluent Society*, *American Capitalism* and *The New Industrial State* by J. K. Galbraith. *The New Industrial State* is copyright 1969 by John Kenneth Galbraith (Hamish Hamilton, London).

Hutchinson Publishing Group, publishers of *Party Games* by Christopher Mayhew.

The Institute of Economic Affairs, publishers of *Economic Fact and Fantasy* by G. C. Allen; *Growth Through Industry*, for extracts from contributions by D. H. Barran, John Jewkes and Richard Lynn; *The National Plan* by John Brunner; *Pricing in Hungary* by Bela Csikos-Nagy; *Agenda for a Free Society* by Arthur Seldon; *Economic Devolution in Eastern Europe* by Ljobo Sirc (in association with Longmans); *The Intellectual in the Market Place* by George Stigler; and *The Business of Capitalism* by Harold Wincott (in association with Longmans).

Michael Joseph Ltd, publishers of *The Case for Capitalism*.

The London School of Economics and Political Science, for an extract from *Our Partnership* by Beatrice Webb.

Macmillan and Company Ltd, publishers of *Politics and Economics*, *The Theory of Economic Policy in English Classical Political Economy*, and *The Economic Basis of Class Conflict*, all by Lionel Robbins; *Conditions of Economic Progress* by Colin Clark; *The General Theory of Employment, Interest and Money* and *The Economic Consequences of the Peace* by J. M. Keynes; *The New Ordeal by Planning* by John Jewkes; and *Economics of Welfare* by A. C. Pigou.

The Macmillan Company of New York, publishers of *Adventures of Ideas* by A. N. Whitehead.

McGraw-Hill Book Company, publishers of *Innovation in Marketing* by Theodore H. Levitt.

The Marshall McLuhan Dew-Line Newsletter.

Martin Secker & Warburg Ltd, publishers of *The Problem of Power* by Lord Radcliffe.

John Murray Ltd, publishers of *Self-Help* by Samuel Smiles (1958 edn.), with an Introduction by Asa Briggs.

National Westminster Bank Ltd, for an extract from the *District Bank Review*, September 1962, No. 143, by C. F. Carter.

Thomas Nelson & Sons Ltd, publishers of *An Outline of Money* by Geoffrey Crowther.

Penguin Books Ltd, publishers of *The British Worker* by Ferdynand Zweig; *What Happened in History* by Gordon Childe; and *The Ethics of Aristotle*, Penguin Classics edition.

Princeton University Press, publishers of *On the Accuracy of Economic Observations* by Oskar Morgenstern (2nd edition, 1963, completely revised).

Professor Joan Robinson for extracts from her *Collected Economic Papers* (Blackwell).

Routledge & Kegan Paul Ltd, publishers of *The Common Sense of Political Economy* by Philip H. Wicksteed (revised edition, 1933); *The Open Society and Its Enemies* by Professor Sir Karl Popper (5th edition, vol. I, p. viii and vol. II, pp. 275 and 348); *The Road to Serfdom* and *The Constitution of Liberty* by F. A. Hayek; *Economic Development of the Overseas Empire* by L. C. A. Knowles.

Acknowledgements

Sidgwick & Jackson Ltd, publishers of *The Under-Privileged Nations* by Pierre Moussa.

The Society of Authors, for the Bernard Shaw Estate, for extracts from *The Intelligent Woman's Guide to Socialism and Capitalism.*

The University of Chicago Press, publishers of *Capitalism and Freedom* by Milton Friedman.

A. P. Watt & Sons, for extracts from *Are These Hardships Necessary?* by Sir Roy Harrod; *Ballads for Broadbrows* by A. P. Herbert; *The Work, Wealth and Happiness of Mankind* and *The New Machiavelli* by H. G. Wells.

C. A. Watts & Co Ltd, publishers of *Economic Philosophy* by Joan Robinson.

Index

Index

K

Index of Authors